10823029

Dior
IN 50 OBJECTS

Illustrations by Francesca Waddell

Published in 2026 by Welbeck
An Imprint of HEADLINE PUBLISHING GROUP LIMITED

1

Cataloguing in Publication Data is available from the British Library

ISBN 9781035430390

Printed and bound in China

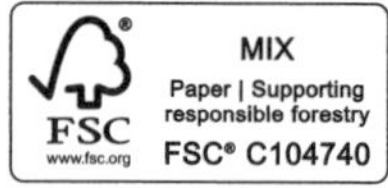

HEADLINE PUBLISHING GROUP LIMITED
An Hachette UK Company
Carmelite House
50 Victoria Embankment
London EC4Y 0DZ

The authorised representative in the EEA is Hachette Ireland,
8 Castlecourt Centre, Dublin 15, D15 XTP3, Ireland (email: info@hbgi.ie)

www.headline.co.uk
www.hachette.co.uk

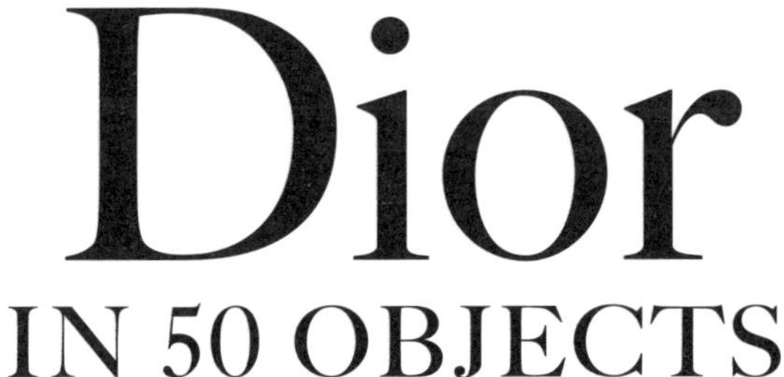

Dior IN 50 OBJECTS

THE ICONIC FASHION HOUSE
THROUGH ITS FINEST CREATIONS

GLENYS JOHNSON

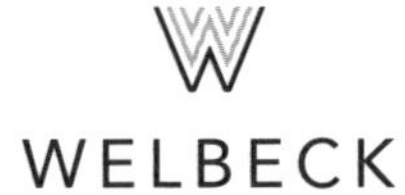

WELBECK

“WHATEVER
YOU DO –
FOR WORK
OR PLEASURE
– DO IT WITH
PASSION!
LIVE WITH
PASSION!”

– Christian Dior,
Little Dictionary of Fashion

CONTENTS

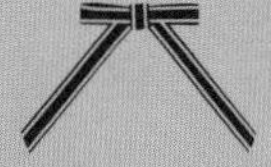

INTRODUCTION

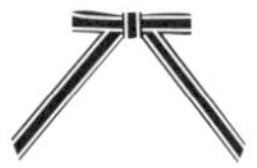

When Christian Dior entered the world in 1905, no one could know he would change the world of fashion forever. As a small child, Christian spent many of his days in the garden of his family's home – referred to as "Les Rhumbs" – in Granville, Normandy. His family was quite comfortable financially, due to Christian's father, Alexandre Louis Maurice Dior, and his successful fertilizer business. His mother, Marie-Madeleine Dior, was known to spend much of her time tending to the flowers and shrubbery surrounding the villa. Christian would later credit this formative time with inspiring many aspects of his work, and florals would become a key aspect of the Dior brand.

The Dior family relocated to Paris in 1910, where Christian would grow up keen to build a career in the art world. In his 20s, Christian would open a small gallery where he worked alongside the likes of surrealists like Salvador Dalí, ultimately having to shut its doors in 1933 due to the impact of the Great Depression. This led Christian into the fashion industry, first by selling fashion sketches to the likes of

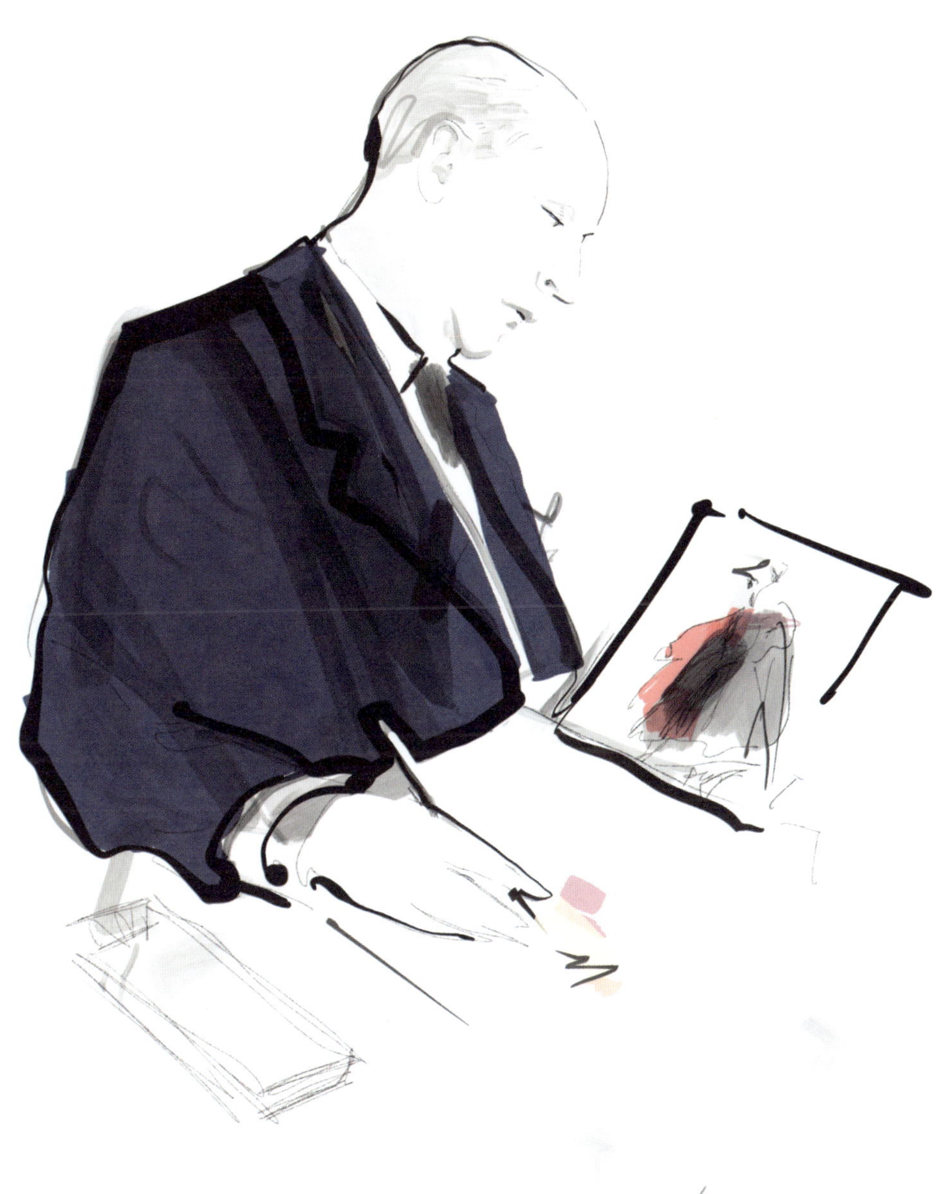

Jean Patou, Schiaparelli and Balenciaga. By 1946, Christian Dior had joined forces with entrepreneur Marcel Boussac to create the couture house of Christian Dior. The waves created by his spring/summer 1947 collection, famously described by Carmel Snow of *Harper's Bazaar* as "such a New Look", were felt throughout the fashion world. The collection is still referenced today as one of the most important developments in the history of fashion.

Since Christian's passing in 1957, Dior has continued to grow and evolve as one of the world's most respected fashion houses in the world. This book takes you through the rich history of Dior through 50 iconic elements that have played critical roles in shaping the essence of the French fashion house. From the symbols that Christian himself saw as lucky charms to show-stopping gowns created by the creative directors that defined their respective eras, each page offers a key piece of the puzzle, forming a picture of the Dior brand, and the visionaries that have reigned as creative director through the maison's illustrious history.

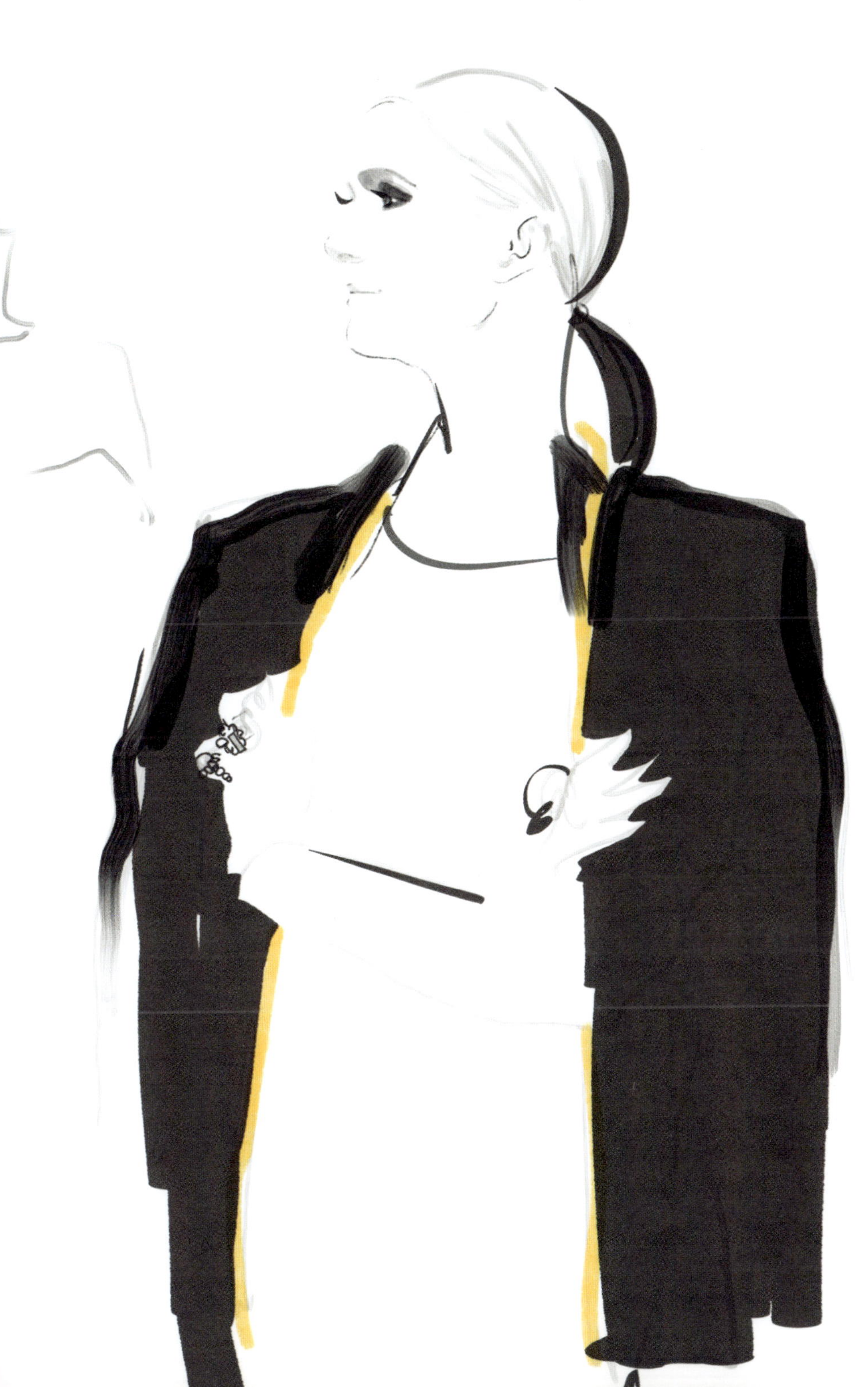

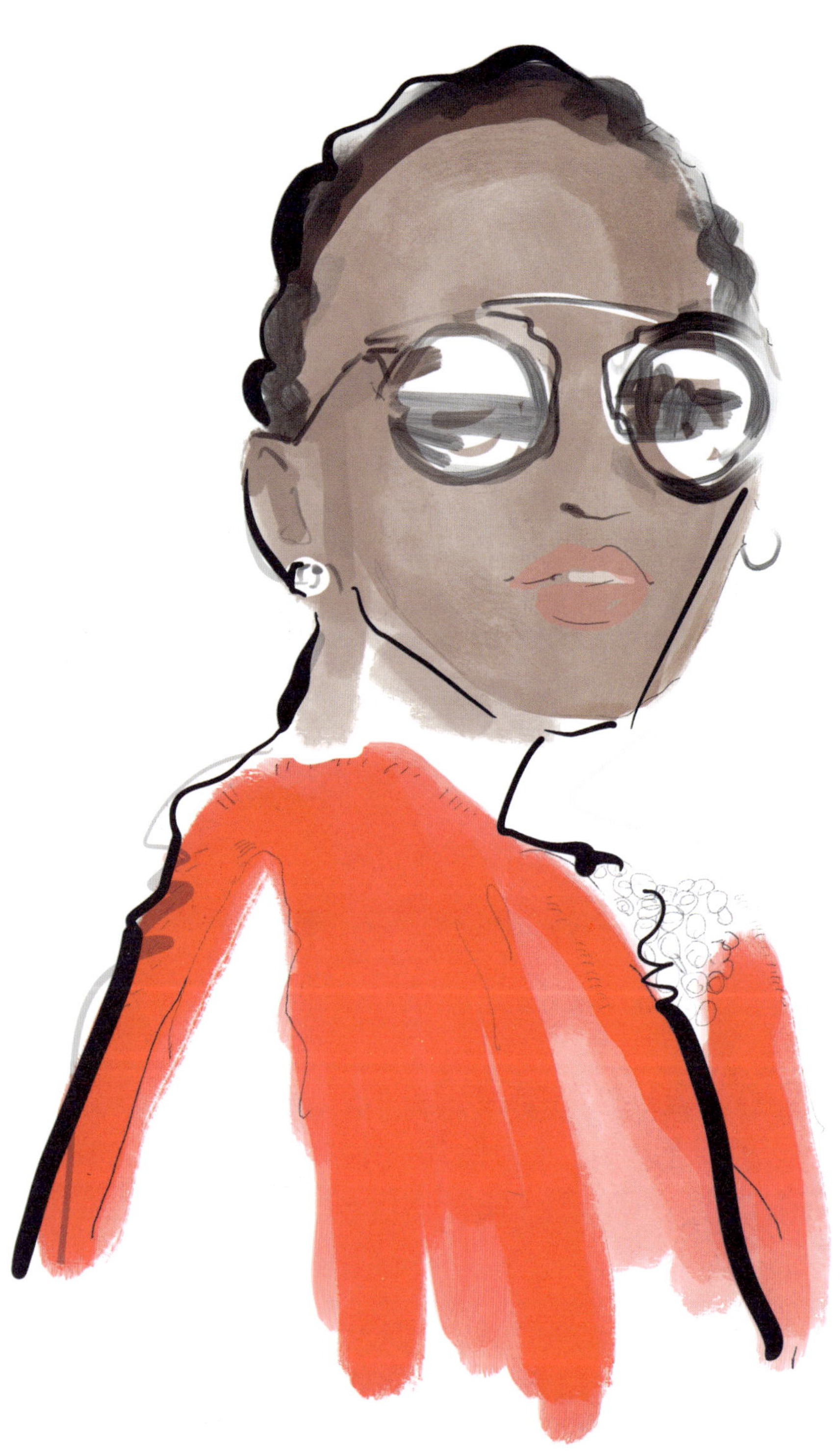

"THE WORLD IS WONDERFULLY FULL OF BEAUTIFUL WOMEN WHOSE SHAPES AND TASTES OFFER AN INEXHAUSTIBLE DIVERSITY. MY COLLECTION MUST CATER TO EACH ONE OF THEM."

– Christian Dior, 1956

1

GRANVILLE

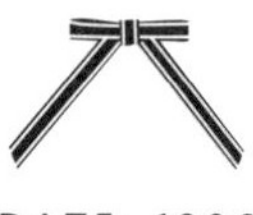

DATE: 1906
LOCATION: NORMANDY, NORTHWEST FRANCE
SIGNIFICANCE: CHILDHOOD HOME OF CHRISTIAN DIOR, NOW THE MUSÉE CHRISTIAN DIOR

For the formative years of Christian Dior's life, from 1906 onwards, he and his family lived in the seaside town of Granville, located in Normandy in the northwest of France. Here, they lived in a Belle Époque-style home they referred to as "Les Rhumbs", which was surrounded by an English-style garden that would inspire the designer throughout his life. In his 1956 autobiography, *Dior by Dior*, Christian recalled, "I have the most tender and amazing memories of the house of my childhood… My life, my style, owe almost everything to its location and its architecture." Though they moved to Paris in 1910 when he was still a young boy, the home remained in the hands of the Dior family and would be the location of many summer holidays.

At just 20 years old, Christian would put his stamp on the family home by redesigning the pond and pergola. Following some financial hardship, the house was sold to the city of Granville in 1932, who opened the garden to the public. But in 1997, it would become once again dedicated to Dior with the opening of the Musée Christian Dior, which, as of 2025, remains a top destination for Dior fans from around the world. The museum has hosted exhibitions including *Dandyisms 1808 to 2008 – From Barbay d'Aurevilly to Christian Dior* and *DIOR, The New Look Revolution* in 2015.

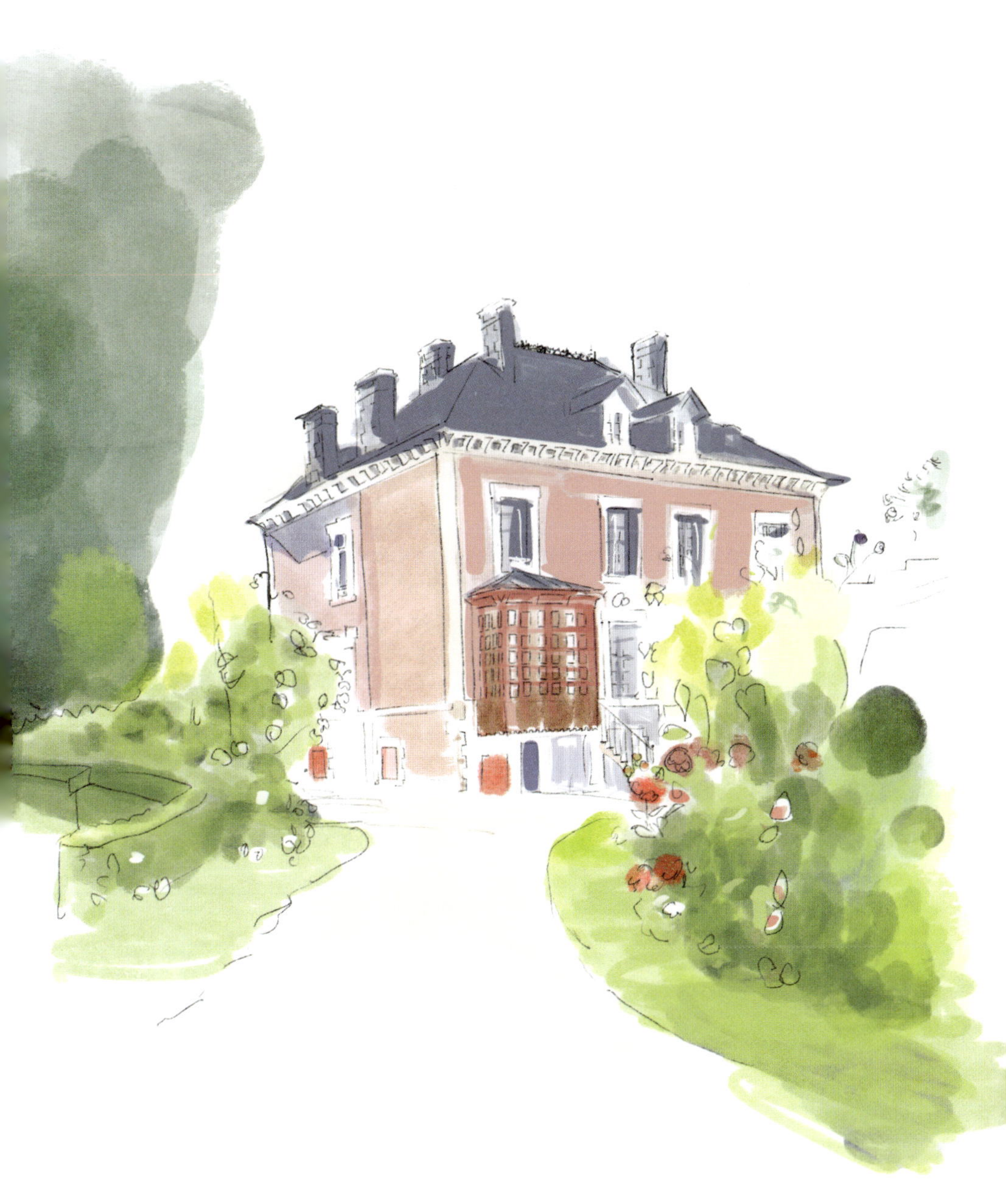

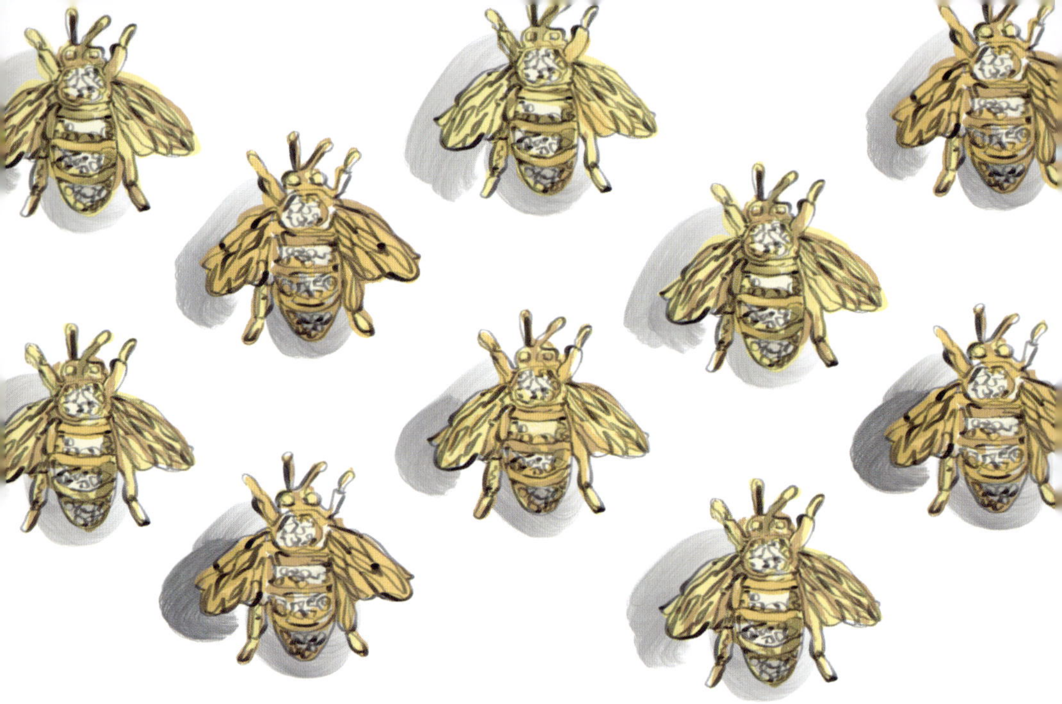

2

BEES

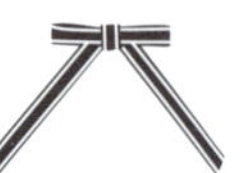

SYMBOLIZES: STRENGTH AND VIGOUR

THE HIVE: CHRISTIAN'S NAME FOR HIS MAISON

APPEARS: ON SADDLE BAG DESIGNS AND GRAPHIC TEES

Christian Dior's superstitious attitude and affinity for floral gardens come together in his love for the humble bumble bee, which he saw as a good luck symbol. In fact, many cultures regard the bee as a symbol of prosperity and positive energy. Beyond incorporating the motif into his designs, Dior was also known to refer to his couture house

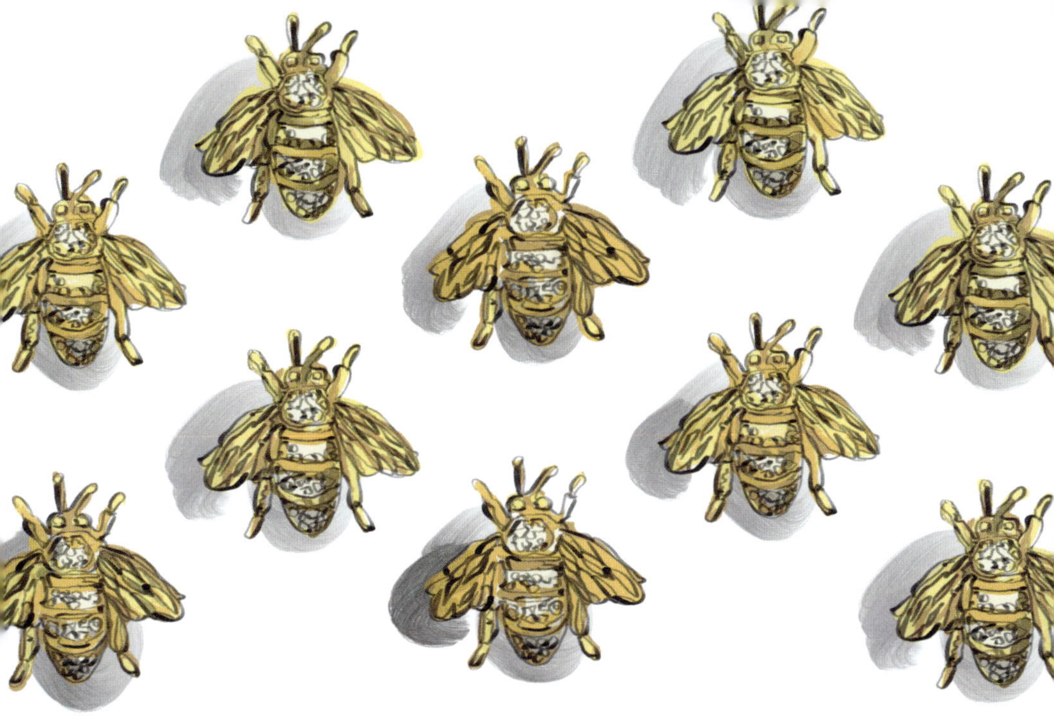

as a “hive” and his fellow workers as “bees”, highlighting its buzzing energy as everyone worked hard to create the collections. It’s said that the Frenchman saw bees as a symbol of strength and vigour, two characteristics he valued for the fashion house.

Over the years, the bee symbol has found its way into various collections across the label, including Hedi Slimane’s dark Dior Homme looks, ready-to-wear womenswear and Dior Joaillerie, which will often use the buzzing insect as the focal point for everything from diamond-encrusted earring studs to pendant necklaces. In 2018, Kim Jones brought in the talents of American artist and designer Kaws to reimagine the bee motif in his signature cartoon-esque style for Jones’ premier Dior collection, a gesture symbolizing the artistic director’s dedication to reviving Dior’s history and reinterpreting for the modern day. The bee emblem was used across some of the fashion house’s most iconic pieces including the saddle bag, while also being the focal point on more everyday styles like graphic tees and zip leather pouches. Today, the Kaws x Dior collection remains a firm favourite among the many fans of Dior’s more streetwear-inspired designs.

3

BUTTERFLIES

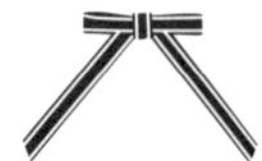

DATE: 1950s TO PRESENT DAY
SIGNIFICANCE: INSPIRATION FROM NATURE
SEEN: ON GARMENTS AND FRAGRANCE PACKAGING

The garden was famously a source of inspiration for Christian Dior, from the vivid colours to the shapes of the flowers, which inspired silhouettes. We can also see that even its winged visitors captured Dior's imagination. Butterflies appeared in Dior collections in the early 1950s, when the colourful insect was depicted on dress designs by Christian Dior himself, and on Dior's footwear styles, created in partnership with esteemed footwear designer Roger Vivier (1907–98).

Butterflies have since appeared in various Dior collections, including former artistic director Maria Grazia Chiuri's cruise 2024 line-up, which displayed butterflies across a wide selection of pieces from the skirts of silk gowns to statement necklaces and handbags. On her Instagram account, looking at the inspiration behind the collection, Chiuri remarks on the symbolism closely linked to the butterfly throughout art and fashion, sharing its ability to represent "metamorphosis, of life, death and rebirth". Butterfly iconography can also be spotted throughout the Dior fragrances, notably in the 2024 release of the La Collection Privée collection, which saw butterflies depicted by Italian artist Pietro Ruffo featured across the marketing campaigns and packaging. This symbol has also been present across Dior's menswear range in various iterations, including Belgian designer Kris Van Assche's butterfly bow-ties and laser-cut shirting and jackets from his 2008 collection, which have come to be a favourite for Dior collectors across the globe.

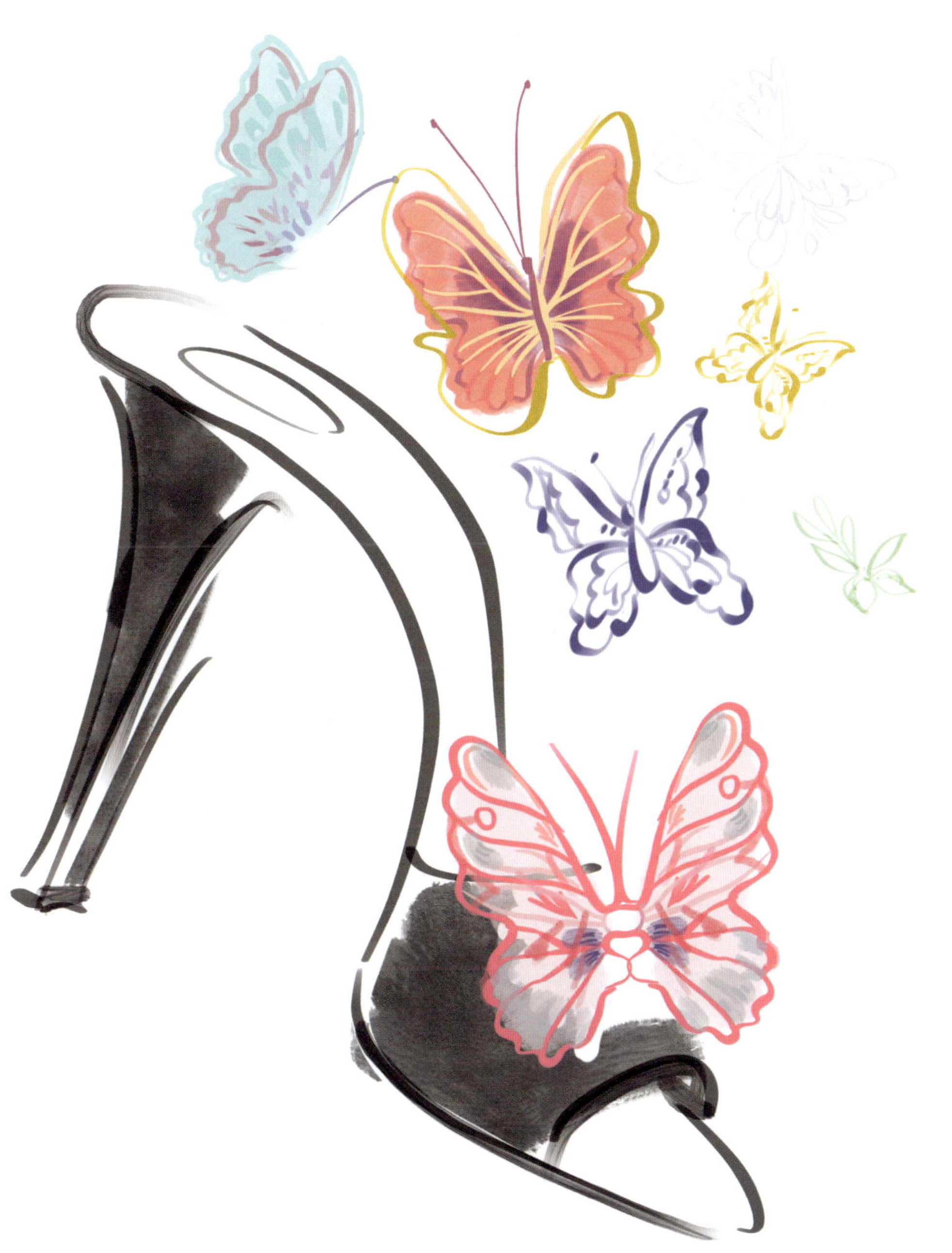

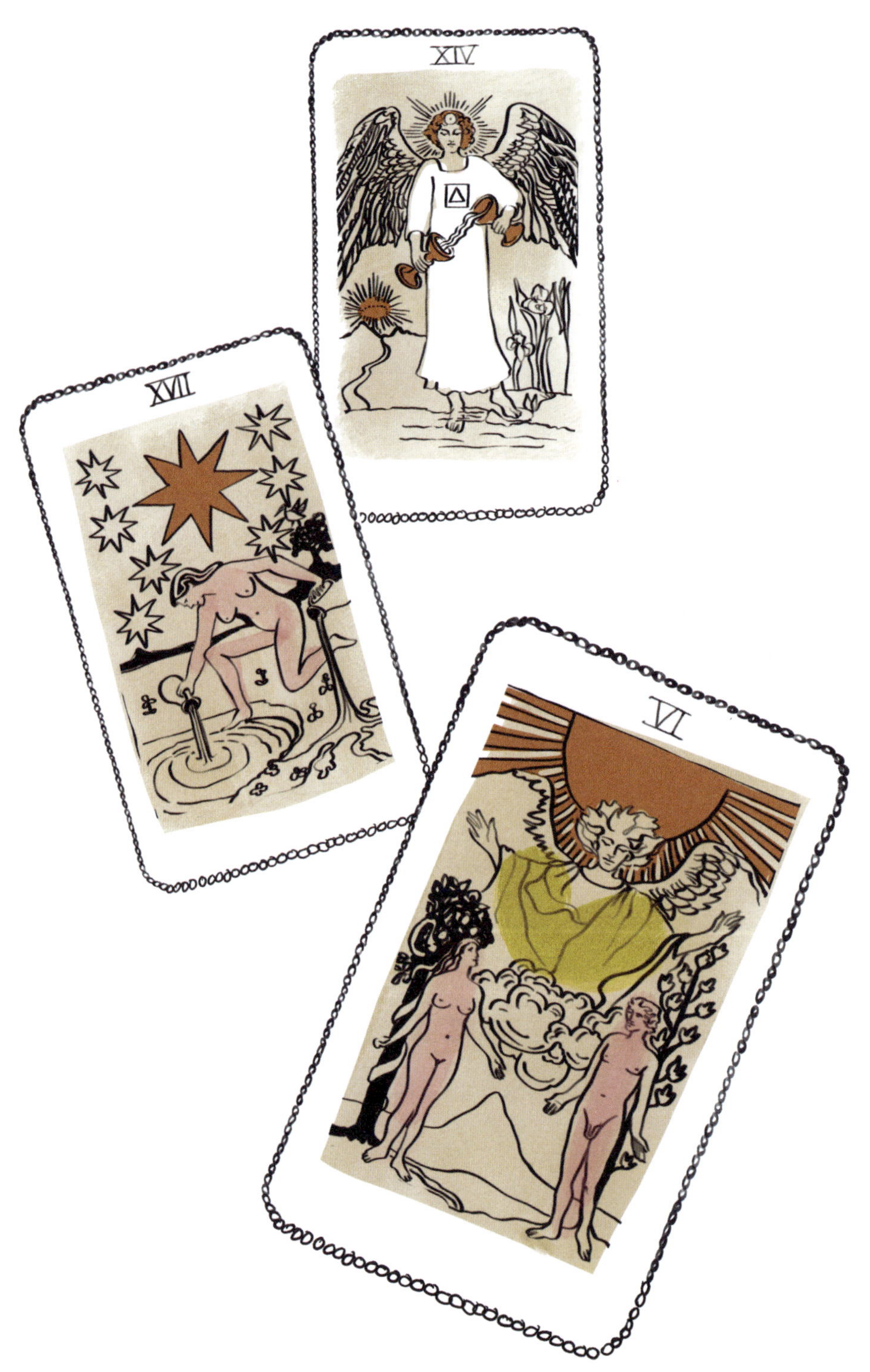
XIV
XVII
VI

4

TAROT

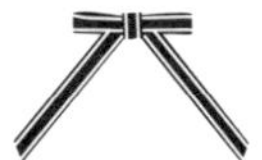

FORTUNE TELLER: MADAME DELAHAYE
INFLUENCED: DIOR'S LIFE AND DESIGNS
INSPIRED: SEVERAL DIOR COLLECTIONS AND DESIGNS OVER THE YEARS

Pierre Cardin, a friend and employee of Christian Dior, once said, "Without her, he did nothing. Nothing, nothing, nothing," when discussing the designer's reliance on the guidance of Madame Delahaye, a French fortune-teller whom Dior was known to visit regularly, taking her guidance very seriously. It's even said that she tried to dissuade him from venturing on his final trip to Italy, where he was to die of a heart attack, aged just 52.

It's reported that Dior's pre-show ritual would often include a visit from Delahaye backstage. Considering this, it's easy to see why tarot imagery and figures continue to be used throughout the fashion house's designs to the present day.

"In times of uncertainty, just like those that Monsieur Dior experienced during the war, any reference to auspicious magic conveys security," Maria Grazia Chiuri told *The New York Times* when presenting the Dior *Le Château du Taro* collection for the spring/summer 2021 season online (when most of the world was experiencing lockdown from the Covid-19 pandemic). The collection took inspiration from various key cards in a traditional tarot deck, including the High Priestess (representing femininity) and Temperance (harmony and balance). Chiuri also noted tarot as inspiration for her collections in 2017 and 2018, which included a range of accessories inspired by the Motherpeace tarot deck, a deck created to focus on the feminine figures often overlooked in traditional tarot decks.

5

ROSES

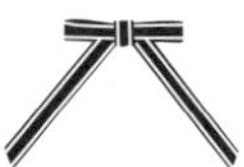

SIGNIFICANCE: EVOKED MEMORIES OF DIOR'S MOTHER
INSPIRED: DIOR'S PHILOSOPHY AND FABRIC PRINTS
LEGACY: GRANVILLE ROSE GARDEN

Ever since he was a child, Christian Dior had a deep love for flowers of all shapes and sizes, but there was one in particular that would prove to be more influential than the rest – the rose. Roses were said to have surrounded Dior's childhood home in Normandy, where his mother, Madeleine Martin, was known to spend much of her time tending to the garden. It's these valued memories that would continue to inspire Dior as he created his fashion label later in his life.

The influence of roses can be seen in various corners of the French fashion house, including Christian's concept of the flower woman (or *femme fleur*), which can be defined as a sort of philosophy that women should be dressed as prettily as a flower and therefore wear pieces that take influence in their shape from nature's florals. Aside from the silhouettes of his dresses, Dior also included his love for roses in his creations through prints of the flower across fabrics, colourways inspired by the red and pink shades of its petals. Rose is also a key scent in a number of Dior fragrances, notably the ever-popular Miss Dior scent launched in 1947.

In 2020, the House of Dior purchased a plot of land in Granville, where they proudly grow approximately 11,000 roses without pesticides and with a strong focus on regenerative agricultural practices (the garden is certified by the Union for Ethical BioTrade/UEBT). Once they're ready to be cultivated, the roses are used in various Dior skincare products.

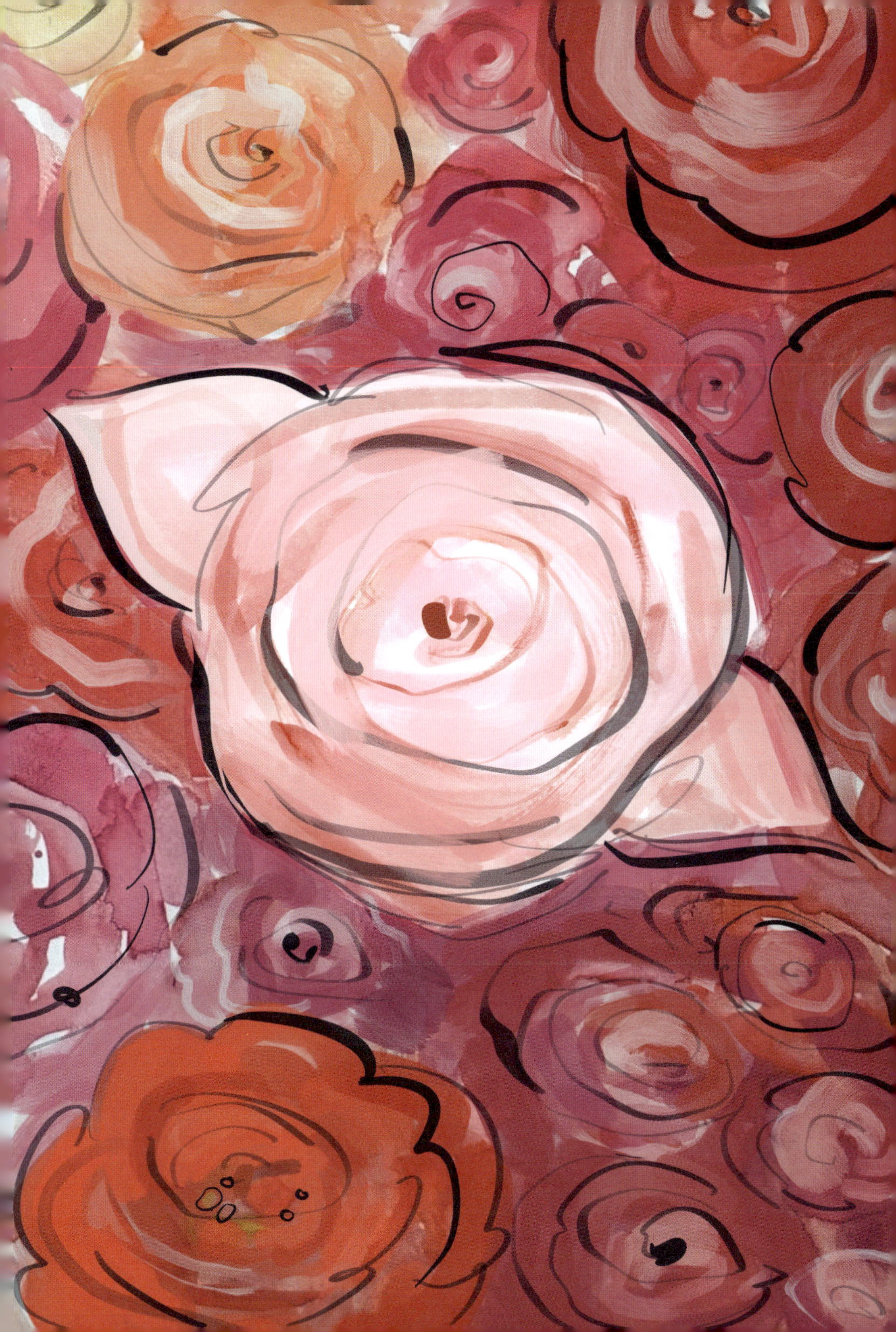

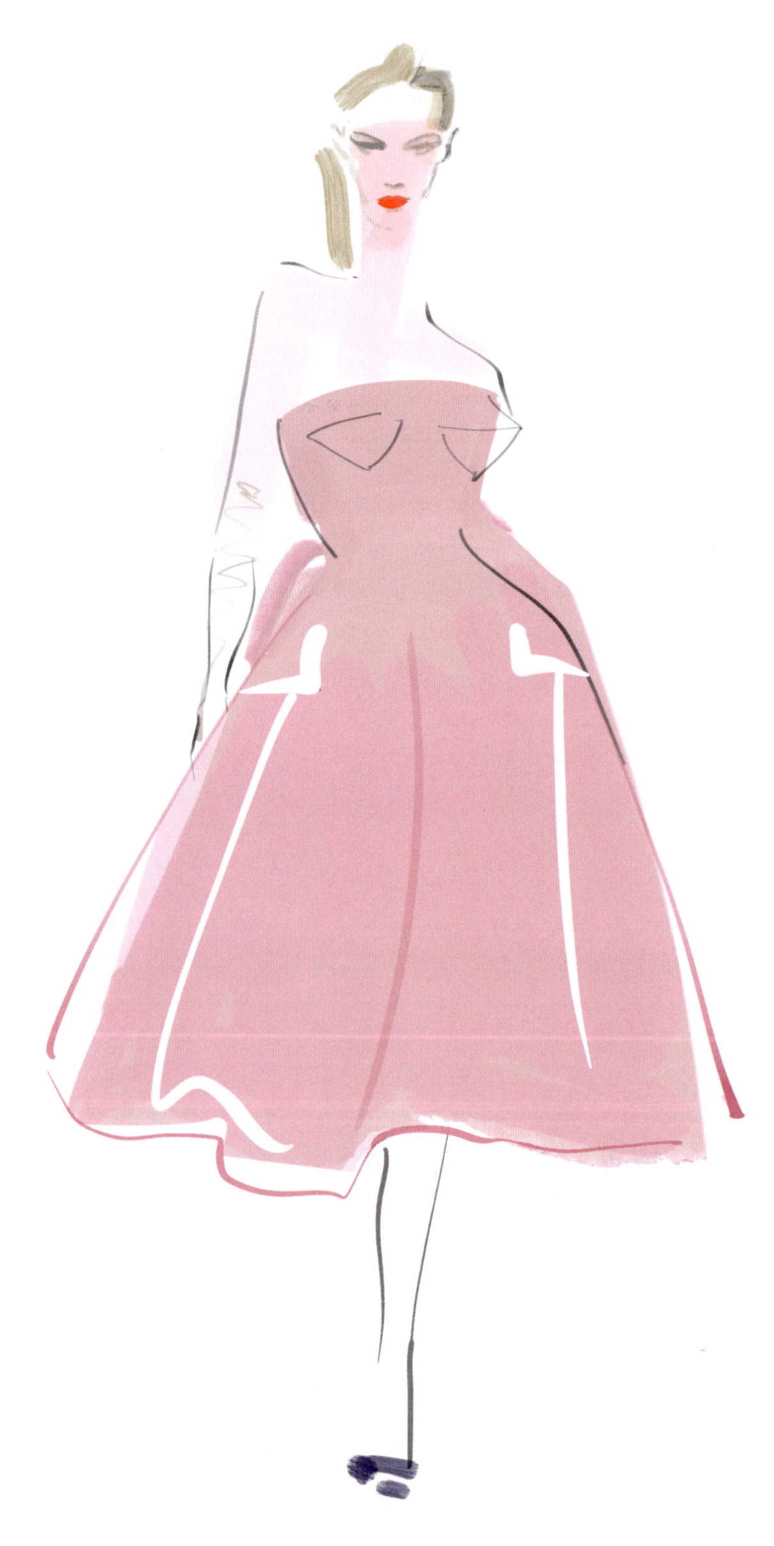

6

PINK

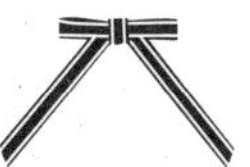

INSPIRED BY: DIOR'S CHILDHOOD IN GRANVILLE
SHADES: ROSE TENDRE, ROSE FRANÇAIS, ROSE BONHEUR
LEGACY: SIGNATURE HOUSE SHADE

Christian Dior's love for the colour pink can be linked back to his childhood home in Granville, referred to as "Les Rhumbs", which was painted a pale pink colour. The house was also famously surrounded by roses and other florals of varying pink hues, so it's little wonder that pink has often been a key colour in almost every Dior collection since its 1947 genesis. Christian would even take to creating his own names for the various pink hues he used: "rose tendre" (tender pink), "rose Français" (French pink) and "rose bonheur" (happy pink) all appeared within the pages of his show notes. Dior famously said: "Every woman should have something pink in her wardrobe. It is the color of happiness and of femininity."

Throughout the fashion house's various iterations, pink has remained a staple colourway for everything from its haute couture outputs to its cosmetic ranges. In the 2016 book, *Dior: The Art of Color*, Dior Cosmetic's creative director, Peter Philips, shared, "A powdery pink is always pretty, but I think that at Dior, there is always room for a daring pink."

Marc Bohan, Dior's creative director from 1961 to 1989, was famously fond of the colour and would make it somewhat of a signature for many of his womenswear designs over this period. Pink would also be the main staple of the Miss Dior ready-to-wear line created by Bohan in 1967, a collection that made such waves it inspired a capsule collection of bright pink vintage-inspired pieces in 2025.

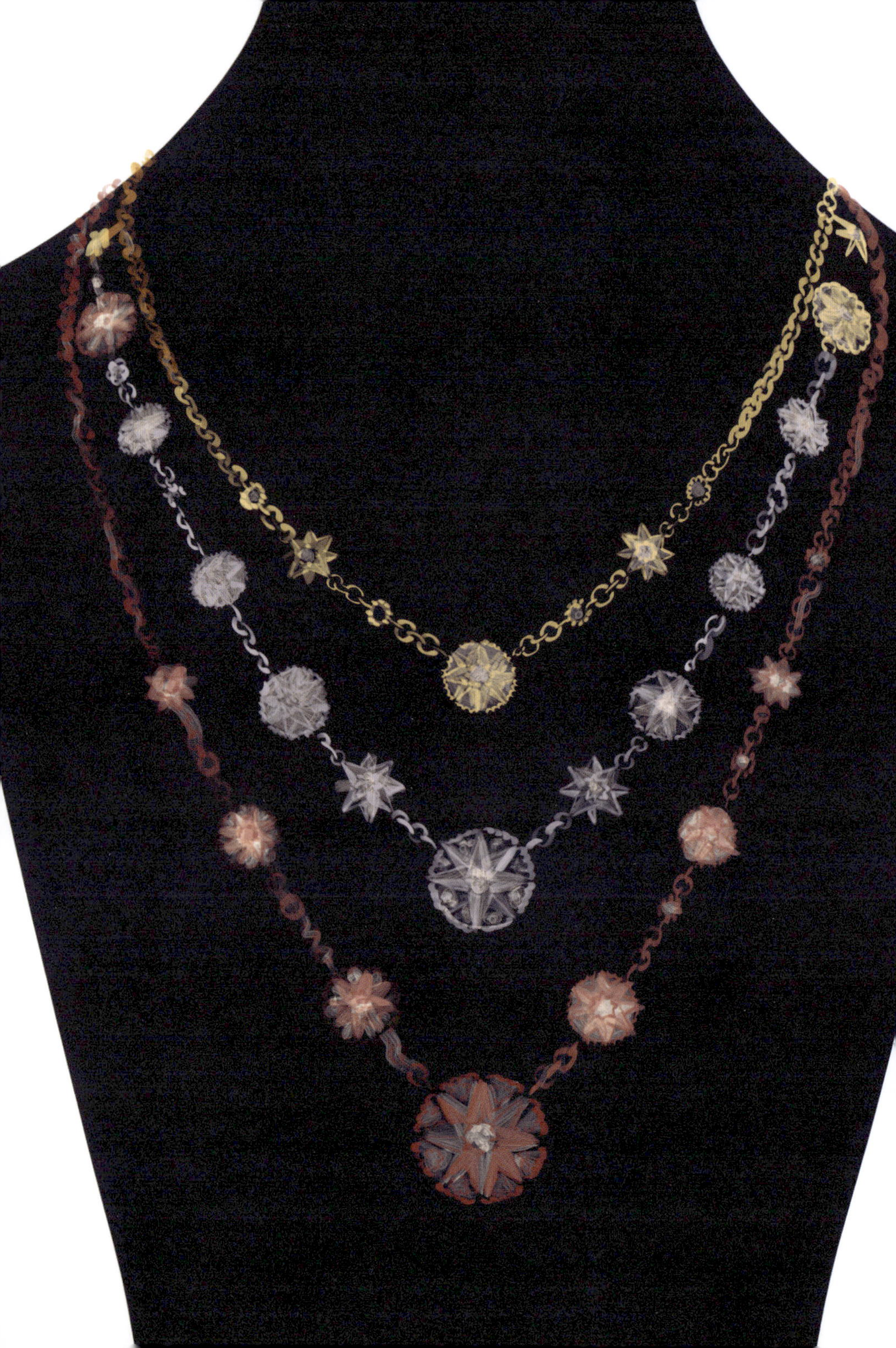

7

STARS

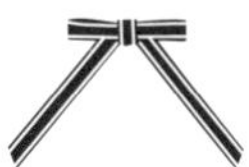

MEANING: DIOR'S GOOD-LUCK CHARM
SEEN ON: JEWELLERY, FRAGRANCE AND COUTURE
LEGACY: DECORATES STOREFRONTS IN HONOUR OF CHRISTIAN DIOR'S SENTIMENT

Christian Dior was known to be a superstitious man throughout his life and as he ventured into launching his namesake label, his keen interest in the mystical world would be a key theme in his designs. Proof of this sentiment can be found in the designer's love for star symbols. The story goes that in April 1946, on his way to meet with French entrepreneur Marcel Boussac, Christian came across a metal star on the street. Dior is said to have seen this as a sign that good things were coming and used it as inspiration for a number of prints, including across the *Bonne Étoile* dress from his 1952 collection.

In 2017, Maria Grazia Chiuri celebrated the House of Dior's 70th birthday with a collection that looked to Christian's affinity for good-luck charms for inspiration, featuring stars on a number of designs. The star continues to remain an important aspect of the Dior brand with the five-point shape appearing across both couture looks and ready-to-wear styles, including its iconic handbags and casual footwear. Dior's lucky star can also be seen throughout the merchandising from the fashion house and adorning the exterior of a number of its brick and mortar locations, displayed to honour Christian Dior's legacy.

8

RED

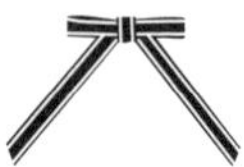

SIGNIFICANCE: A STRATEGIC BURST OF COLOUR ON THE RUNWAY
SYMBOLIZES: PASSION, CONTROL, ENERGY, LIFE
LEGACY: REMAINS A KEY COLOUR ACROSS APPAREL, ACCESSORIES AND COSMETICS

Rich red hues were an important colour for Christian Dior throughout his life and would notably be used as what the designer would refer to as "un coup de Trafalgar", a strategic burst of colour on the runway to captivate the audience of his shows. His first collection for the Dior autumn/winter 1947 season saw looks such as the aptly titled "rouge éclatant" and "rouge satan" open the event. In his book *The Little Dictionary of Fashion*, Dior shared tips for wearing the hue: "There is certainly a red for everyone; and if you do not choose to have a whole frock or suit of red, then you may use it instead for accessories – a red hat to wear with an all-black or gray outfit is good; or a red cravat of heavy silk with a cream frock; or a red umbrella with a gray coat."

Though pinks and greys are often referred to as "the Dior colours", red was undeniably critical in forming the Dior brand – and remains so to this day. John Galliano notably dedicated an entire Christian Dior spring/summer 2006 couture line (and corresponding runway show) to the colour, while creative director of Dior beauty, Peter Philips, has ensured the power of red is infused into Dior beauty wherever possible. In *Dior: The Art of Color*, Philips shared, "I adore red and since my first day at Dior I've always used red [...] It may well be the color of passion, but it's also a controlled color. In makeup, red lipstick has to be applied perfectly. A woman who wears red lipstick eats with control, speaks with control and even controls her kisses. Red is a contradiction."

"Red is a very energetic and beneficial color. It is the color of life. I love red and I think it suits almost every complexion"

Christian Dior

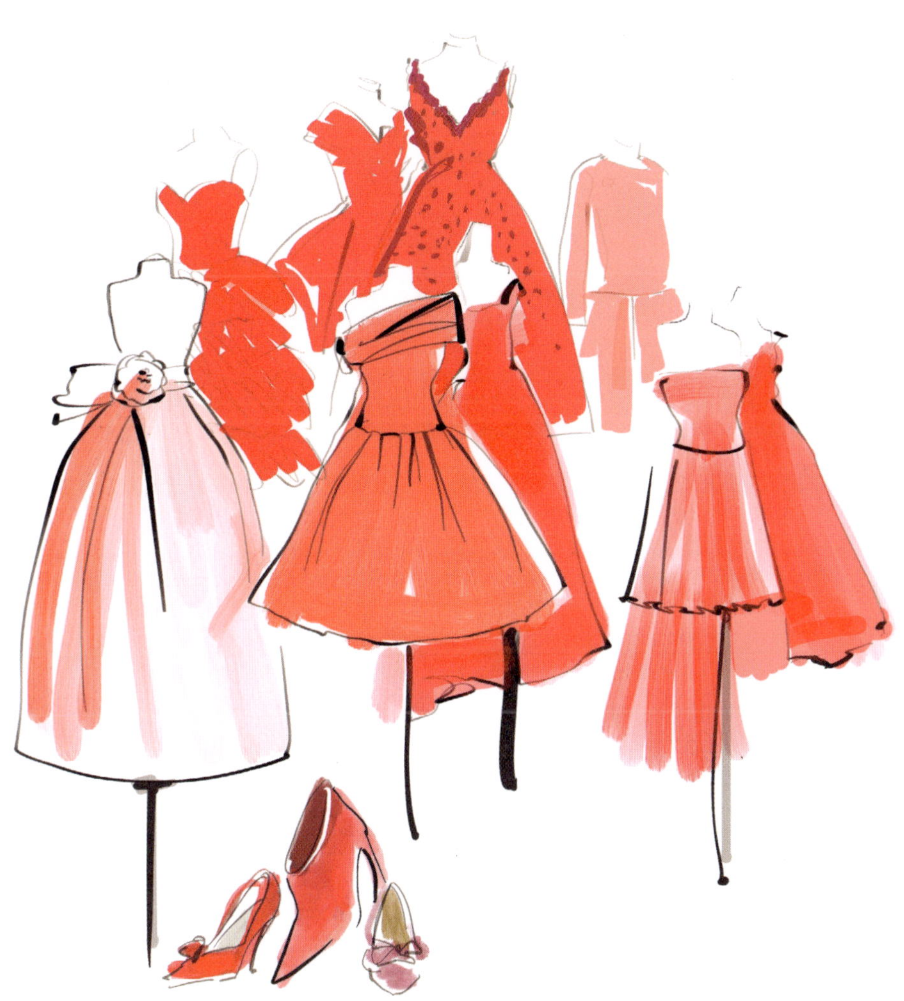

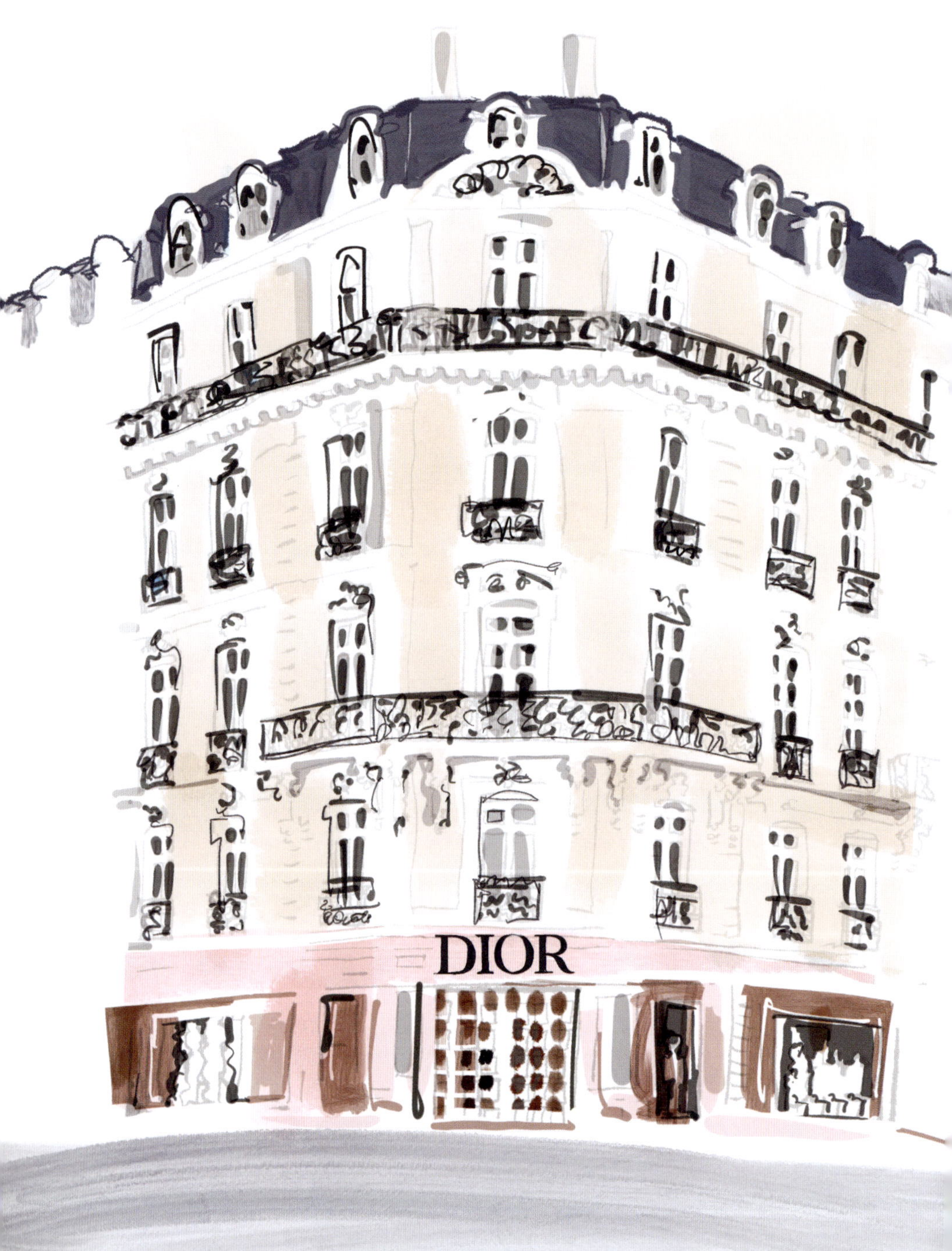
DIOR

9

30 MONTAIGNE

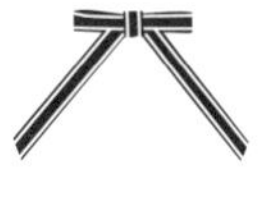

DATE: 1946

LOCATION: 8TH ARRONDISSEMENT, PARIS

SIGNIFICANCE: DIOR'S FIRST AND FLAGSHIP ATELIER

Rarely does a fashion house have a flagship address so iconic as that of Dior's 30 Montaigne. "It had to be 30 Avenue Montaigne. I was going to settle here and nowhere else!" Monsieur Dior declared, recalling his feelings when discovering the space in 1946. The Paris address was quickly transformed into the home for Dior's new venture, hosting his first runway show in February 1947. Now sprawling across 21,500 square feet, this iconic space has expanded significantly over the years, engulfing a total of eight of its neighbouring buildings.

Dior was known to refer to it as his "hive" and would often welcome his most cherished clients, including Jean Cocteau and Marlene Dietrich, to visit. In 2018, then CEO Pietro Beccari decided that 30 Montaigne was to be transformed to further reflect the importance of the building and its relevance to not only the history of Dior but that of Paris and the wider world of fashion. Beccari brought in the talents of the American architect Peter Marino to refresh the address with a new energy across boutique areas, a restaurant, pâtisserie, gallery spaces and three gardens full of some of Dior's favourite flowers. The project took over two years to complete before it reopened to the public in 2022. The iconic Parisian location now attracts visitors from across the globe, who come to experience a glimpse into the world of Dior like never before.

10

THE BAR SUIT

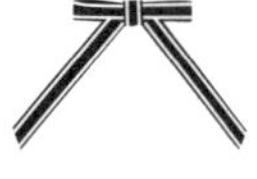

DATE: 1947

STYLE: TAILORED JACKET AND FULL SKIRT

FABRIC: SILK SHANTUNG, WOOL CRÊPE, TAFFETA

It was 1947 when the fashion landscape would be revolutionized with the introduction of Christian Dior's remarkable "New Look". The womenswear collection marked a shift towards a post-war world where women's wardrobes could move beyond the uniformity dictated by fabric rations and the gloom of the Second World War. But not everyone would be so keen to embrace the new era and its playful fashions.

Dior's 1947 collection (officially titled *La ligne corolle*) showcased a number of looks that used what many considered excess fabric, often resulting in longer and fuller skirts than the humble styles dominating the era. Soon the "Little-Below-the-Knee-Club" group would appear to protest at Dior's designs, with some members even physically attacking women wearing Dior. One of the key looks from the collection was the "Bar Suit", a two-piece style featuring a sharply tailored jacket designed to sculpt to the feminine figure. The rumour goes that the jacket even featured wool padding to keep the dramatic shape in place. In *Dior on Dior*, Christian states, "I think of my work as ephemeral architecture, dedicated to the beauty of the female body."

The ivory jacket was crafted from silk shantung while the skirt was a pleated wool crêpe with a structured taffeta petticoat. The Bar Suit was a favourite look of Monsieur Dior himself, who incorporated various versions of the outfit into nearly all of his collections. Many of his successors have also reinterpreted the Bar Suit to reflect their respective periods, proving the power of Dior's innovative 1940s look.

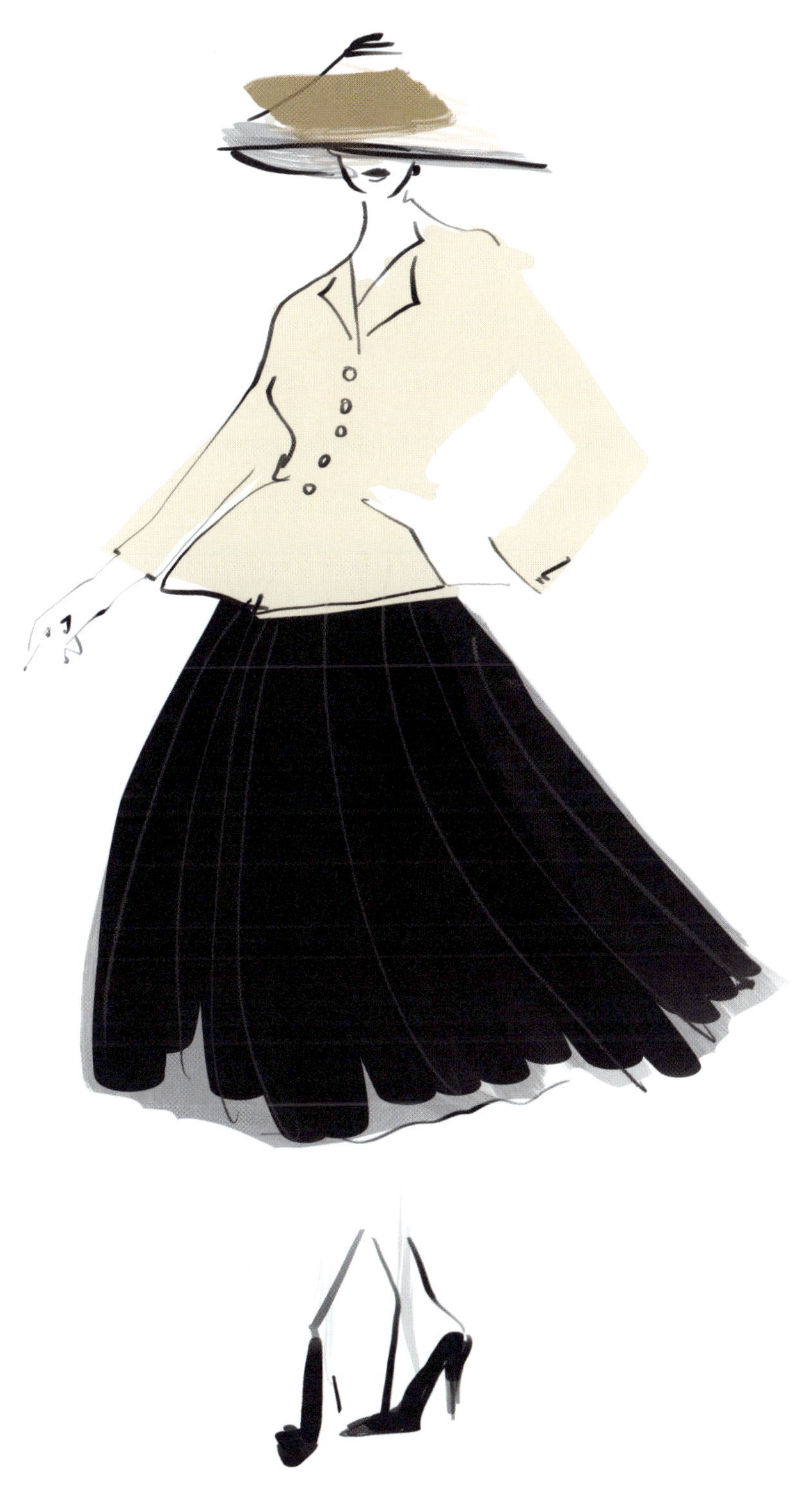

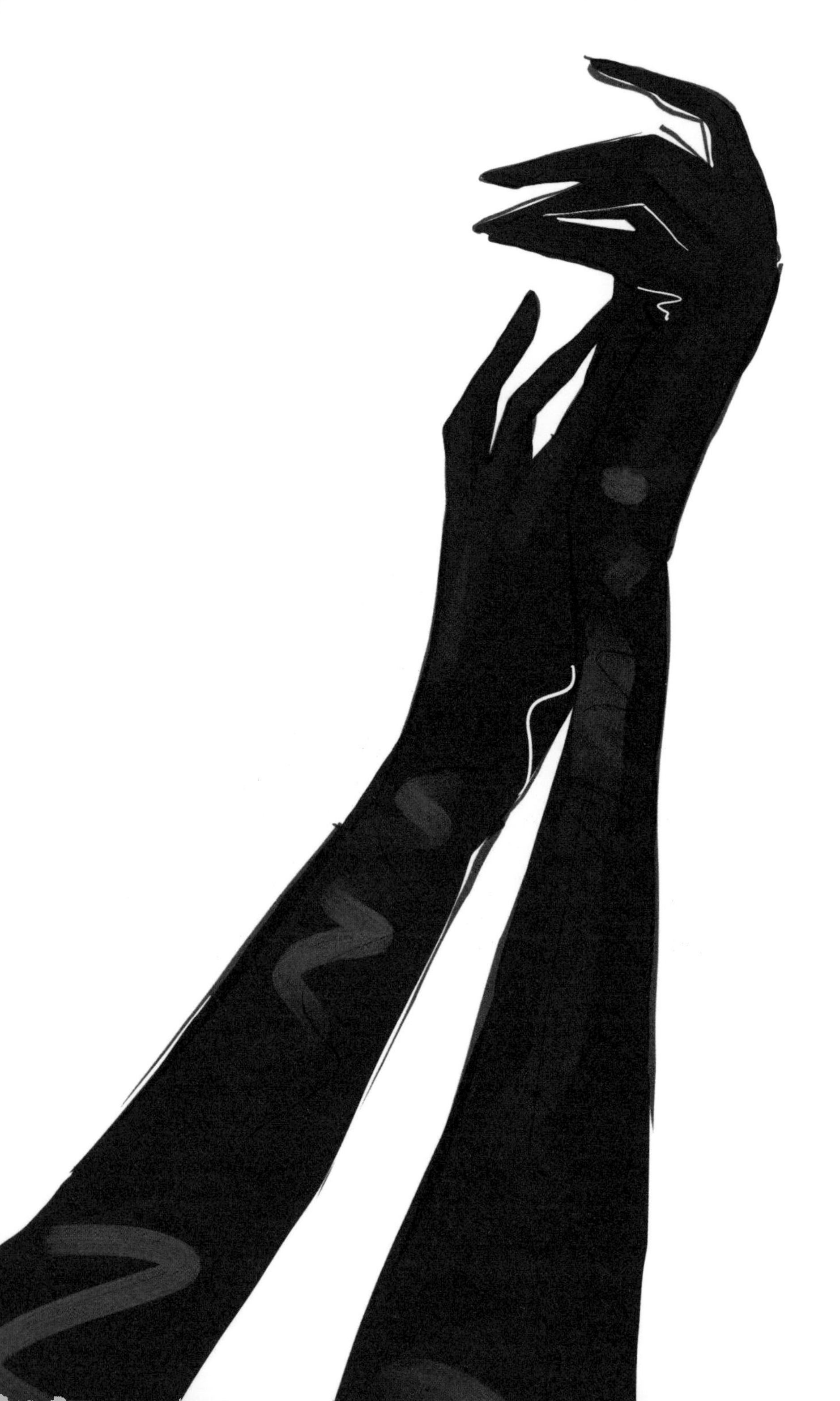

11

GLOVES

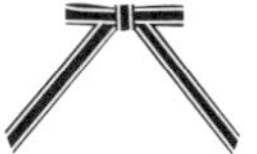

DATE: FROM FIRST 1945 COLLECTION ONWARDS
CODES: ELEGANCE, SOPHISTICATION, FEMININITY
IMPACT: CONTRAST, ELONGATION, COMPLETION OF THE LOOK

Alongside Christian Dior's controversial hemlines that came with his New Look collection in 1947, the designer would use another tactic that nudged women into more feminine dress during this era.

Gloves were used to complement Dior's dresses as early as the Frenchman's very first collection, presented in the Dior salon in Paris, in February 1945. They played a key part in Dior's dedication to creating a full head-to-toe look for women following the Second World War and were seen to communicate both elegance and sophistication, two characteristics often seen as frivolous just months earlier. Throughout the late 1940s and through the 50s, gloves were depicted as an essential accessory across *Vogue* features displaying Dior looks – from designs that climbed the arms styled alongside mink cuff gowns in 1954 to white driving gloves in an issue from 1958.

In the now-iconic photographs by German photographer Willy Maywald (1907–85), model Renee Barton can be seen wearing long black gloves that contrast with the Bar Suit. Gloves remain a mainstay for plenty of Dior's haute couture looks, making appearances in looks from delicate floral-embroidered mesh in Maria Grazia Chiuri's spring/summer 2013 collection to actor and Dior ambassador Anya Taylor-Joy, wearing beaded opera gloves to a Dior event in 2022. And if the spring/summer 2025 collection is anything to go by (Dior's "Tribales" gloves took centre stage with their stretch lambskin construction that sits upon the shoulder), gloves will be forever synonymous with the maison.

12

LEOPARD PRINT

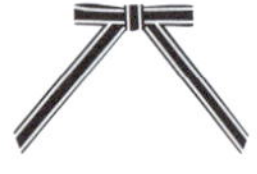

DATE: 1947

INSPIRATION: MITZAH BRICARD, DIOR'S FRIEND AND MUSE

UTILIZED: DRESSES, TRENCH COATS, BAGS AND COSMETICS PACKAGING

Although we know that animal skins worn as clothing long predate the birth of the fashion industry, Christian Dior's 1947 collection did wonders for bringing one particular style to haute couture.

"If you're fair and sweet, don't wear it," Dior said of the leopard-print designs featured in his debut apparel collection. This would be the first time that the world had seen the print used in a fashion collection outside of fur styles. Dior wrote about the print in his autobiography, *Dior by Dior*, "I thought that such a unique nature, with its inimitable excesses, would wonderfully balance the overly cautious nature which I owe to my Norman roots."

The incorporation of the feline-inspired look was without doubt a nod to Christian's close friend and muse Mitzah Bricard, who was famously fond of the spotted style. Leopard has remained an important motif for the French fashion house with each artistic director putting their own spin on the print. Gianfranco Ferré created head-to-toe looks that excluded his love for Italian-style excess, while John Galliano was known to infuse the print into many of his theatrical designs. Fast forward to the present day and leopard print is still a mainstay across many Dior collections, from trench coats on the autumn/winter 2024 runway to the iconic "Book Tote", to a limited-edition cosmetics line adorned with the feline spots.

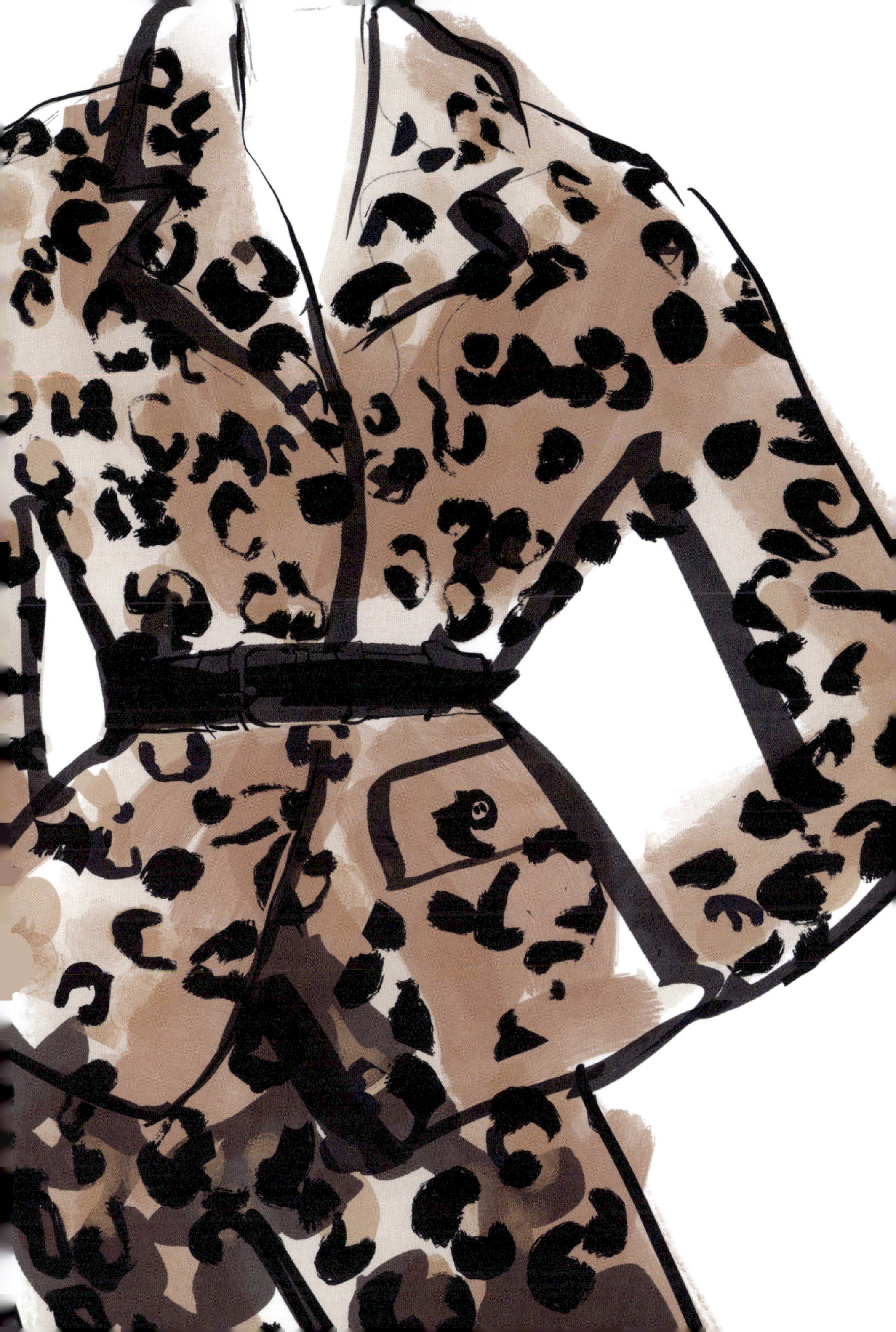

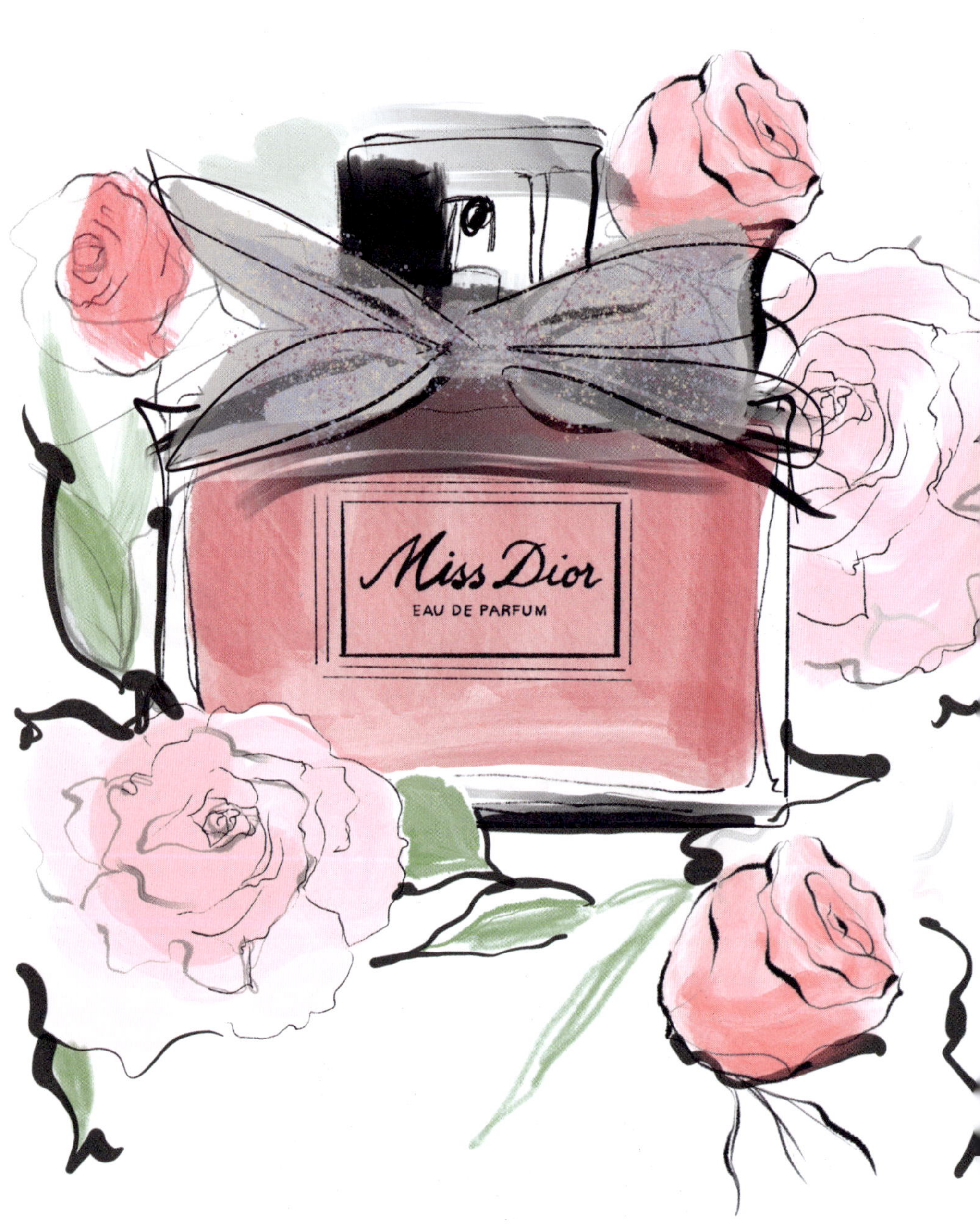
Miss Dior
EAU DE PARFUM

13

MISS DIOR

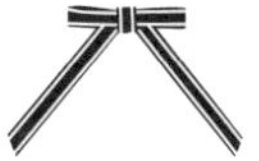

DATE: 1947
CREATED BY: CHRISTIAN DIOR / PAUL VACHER / JEAN CARLES
FRAGRANCE: JASMINE, NARCISSUS, NEROLI AND ROSE

In 1947, Christian Dior thought it time to delve into the world of fragrance and called upon the talents of perfumers Paul Vacher and Jean Carles to create the first Dior perfume. The story goes that Christian set out to create "a perfume that smells like love" and was inspired by the unwavering strength of Catherine, his sister. Catherine Dior was a freedom fighter with the French Resistance who spent a period in a concentration camp before successfully fleeing and returning to safety in France. She then opted for a quieter life and dedicated her days to selling flowers at the local market. It was one of Christian's key collaborators, Mitzah Bricard, who would come up with the name of the perfume, however, as she is said to have exclaimed, "Here comes Miss Dior!" when Catherine entered the Dior studio.

Since its launch in 1947, the eau de parfum has become a signature Dior scent, with wearers admiring the blend of jasmine, narcissus, neroli and rose presented with base notes of patchouli, oak and sandalwood. The fragrance has inspired various other formulas including the Miss Dior Chérie, which launched in 2005. The perfume also inspired a 2021 exhibition which explored the fragrance and its history, hosted at La Colle Noire, Christian Dior's famous château in the south of France.

14

HOUNDSTOOTH

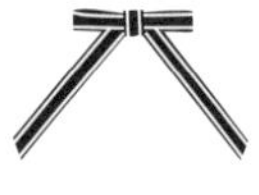

DATE: 1948

SIGNIFICANCE: THE FIRST RUNWAY APPEARANCE OF THE PRINT WAS BY CHRISTIAN DIOR

LEGACY: HAS BEEN REINVENTED IN RECENT COLLECTIONS BY GALLIANO AND KIM JONES

In 1948 Christian Dior introduced the fashion world to yet another pattern previously unseen on the catwalk. Though the history of houndstooth dates back much further, Dior brought the woven material to couture in a way that had fashion-forward women across the globe wanting houndstooth in their wardrobes.

Houndstooth (or *pied-de-poule* in French, translating to "hen's foot") appeared in a number of two-piece styles in Dior's earliest collections before becoming widely associated with one of the label's most iconic fragrances, Miss Dior. The pattern was etched into the side of the perfume bottle and printed across the label and packaging. This played a key role in promoting houndstooth as a luxury pattern, a stark shift away from its roots in utilitarian outerwear styles across northern Europe.

In the 1950s houndstooth began to pick up speed as a coveted style and Dior continued to offer it across its designs, including footwear styles created by Roger Vivier. While at Dior from 2012–15, Raf Simons also brought the signature motif to his footwear styles, most famously with his updated take on the iconic comma heel in 2013. John Galliano was known to enlarge the print in his designs throughout the late 90s and 00s, while Kim Jones preferred a micro version for an understated approach throughout his Dior Men creations.

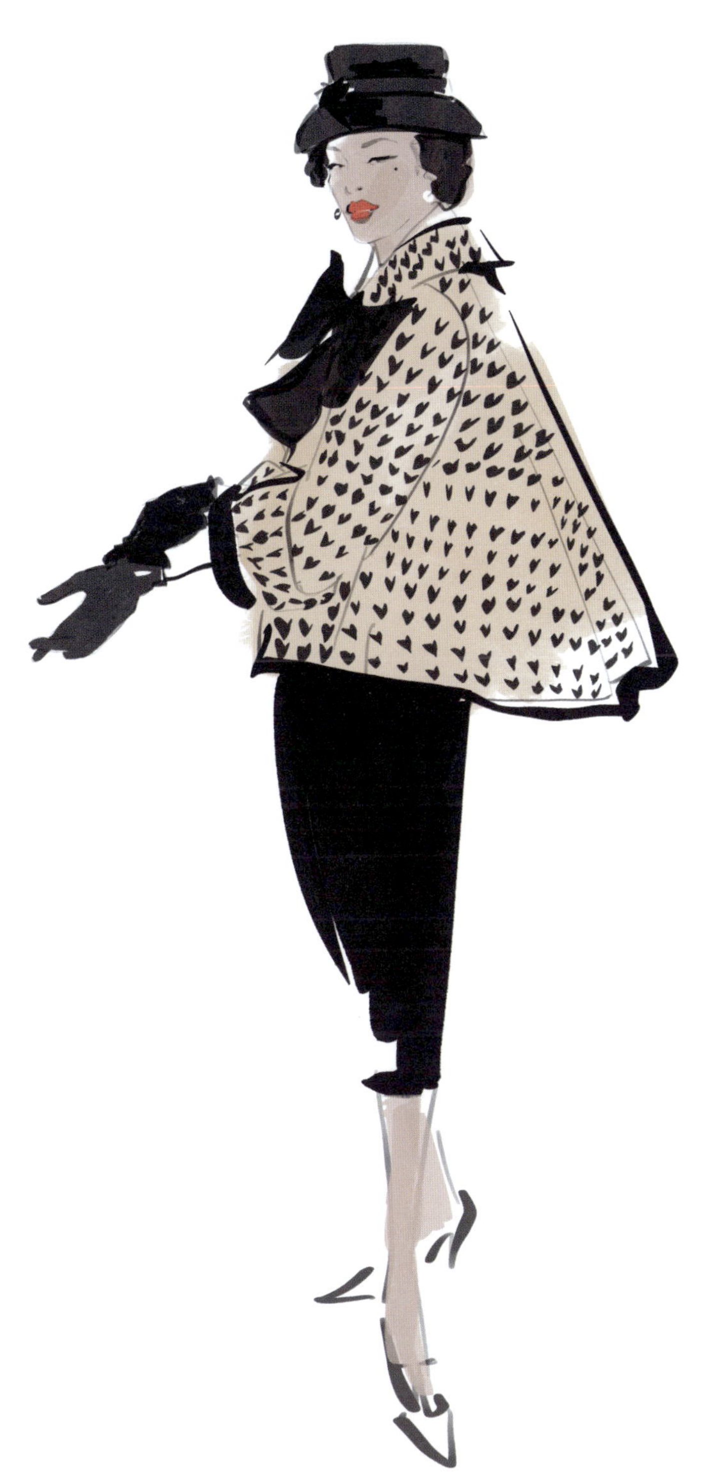

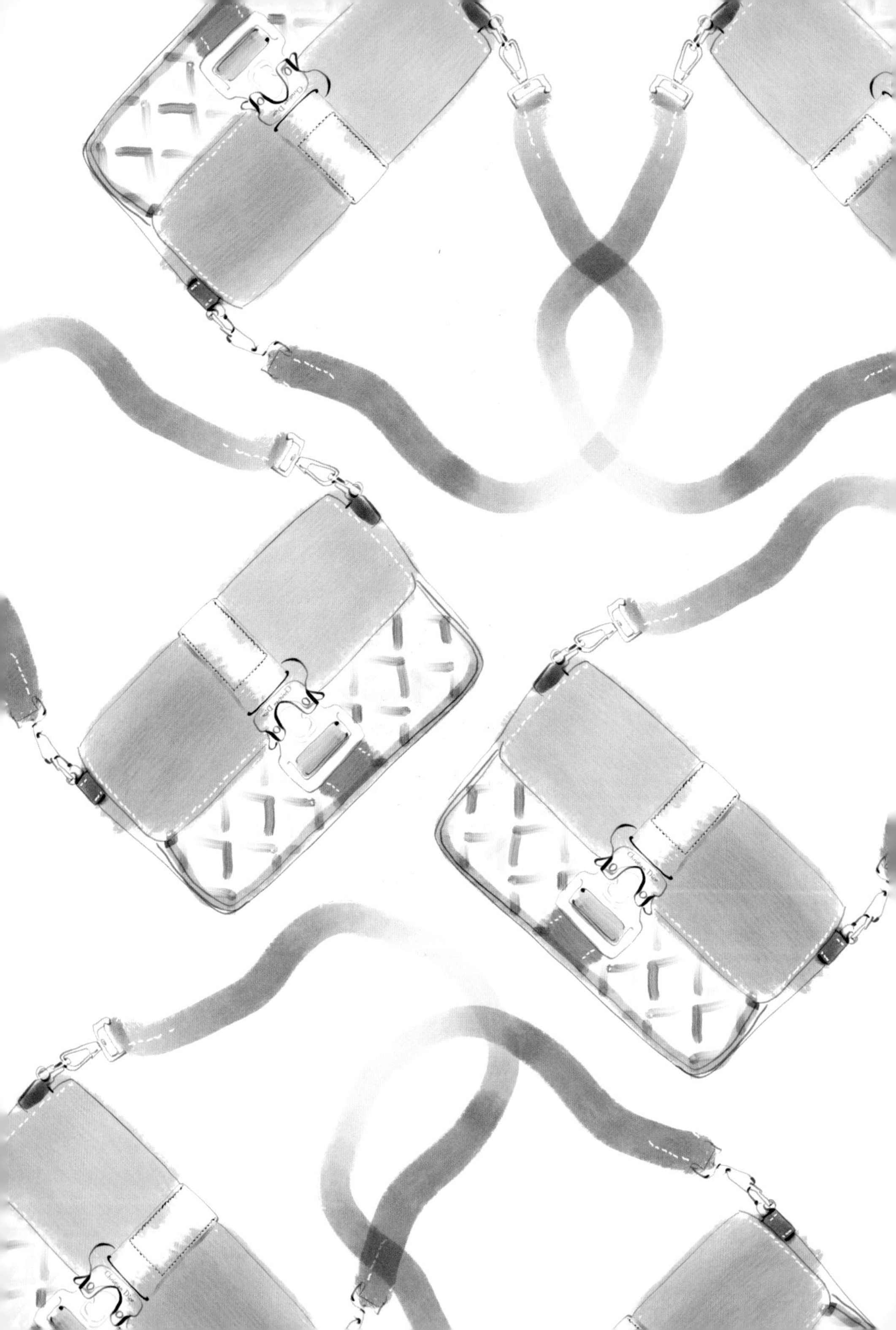

14

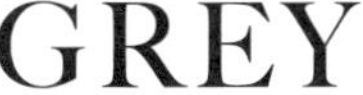

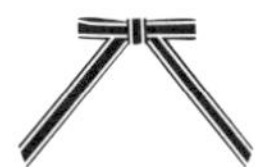

SIGNIFICANCE: A REMINDER OF CLOUDY PARIS SKIES
UTILIZED: AN ESSENTIAL NEUTRAL COLOUR FOR ELEGANCE
VARIATIONS: SHADES INCLUDE "MOTH GREY", "LITTLE GREY DAYS" AND "TRIANON GREY"

Christian Dior referred to grey, in his *Little Dictionary of Fashion*, as "the most convenient, useful and elegant neutral color. [...] If it suits your complexion, there is nothing more elegant than a wonderful, gray satin evening dress. Almost anything goes with gray." Grey is also said to have been representative of Paris due to the cloudy skies of the French capital, and also referenced the grey gravel stones that surrounded his childhood home in Normandy.

Monsieur Dior used plenty of grey shades throughout his collections, including shades he referred to as "moth grey" and "grey little days". His love for grey is also evident in the famous 30 Avenue Montaigne headquarters of the House of Dior, where "Trianon grey" covers the walls and has since inspired the packaging of various cosmetics and accessories across the Dior catalogue. The signature colour notably received attention under the stewardship of Kim Jones, who brought Trianon grey (or sometimes called Montague grey) to life in a number of Dior Men accessories throughout his tenure from 2018 to 2025. The colour has become instantly recognizable to fashion lovers across the globe as a shade emitting sleek sophistication and the essence of Dior.

16

MADAM BRICARD

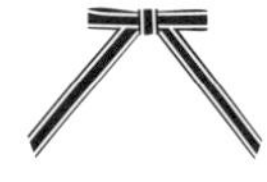

DATE: 1946

RELATIONSHIP: FRIEND AND MUSE

SIGNIFICANCE: INSPIRED DIOR TO INCORPORATE LEOPARD PRINT AND THE COLOUR LILAC INTO HIS DESIGNS

Christian Dior was known to be often surrounded by scores of elegant women wherever he went, from Hollywood starlets to his most cherished models. But there was one woman who was always seen as a cut above the rest – Madame Mitzah Bricard. Dior notably referred to her as a woman "who make[s] elegance their sole raison d'être".

Given the name Germaine Louise Neustadt on her birth in Paris, 1900, the Parisian muse would marry twice in her life, once to a Romanian diplomat, Alexandro Bianco, and then to the president of B.L.B. Laboratories, Hubert Bricard. In 1946 she joined Dior as a pattern-maker, but to assume she would operate in a similar way to her shear-wielding colleagues would be a mistake. The stories go that Bricard rarely made an appearance in the cutting room before noon and would never appear without pearls and an outfit so glamorous, it prompted comments from Dior himself: "Mizza, I wonder whether you might be too dressed up for tea with the Queen of England!" he was said to observe.

Many of Mitzah's outfits incorporated leopard print and the colour lilac, inspiring Dior to adopt them into many of the house's designs. But Bricard's influence on Dior didn't end with Christian's untimely death from a heart attack in 1957. The House of Dior has released a number of designs and collections influenced by the Parisian style icon, including a limited-edition leopard-print scarf and a 2023 cosmetics collection featuring the animal print adorning its sleek packaging.

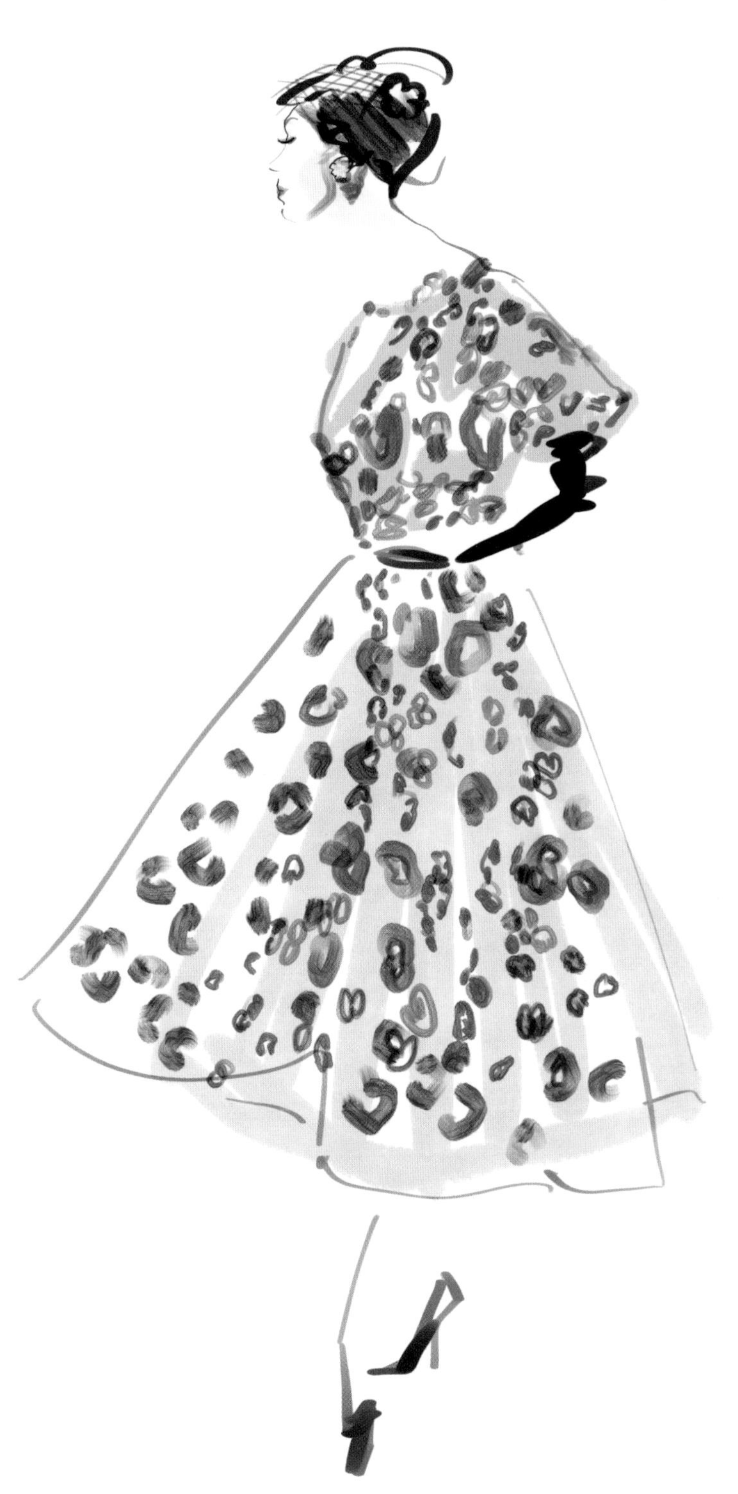

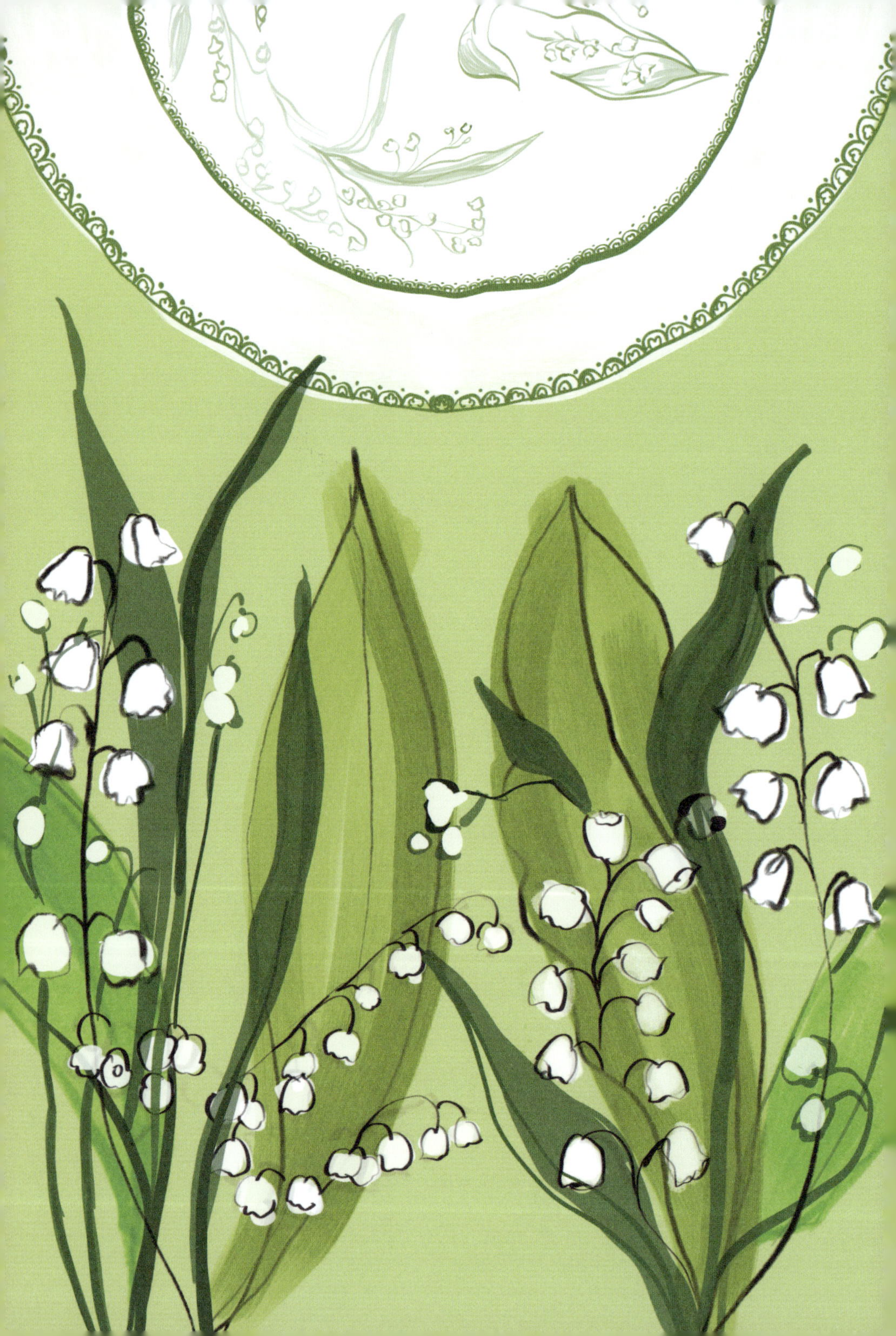

17

LILY OF THE VALLEY

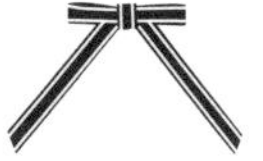

DATE: 1947–PRESENT
SIGNIFICANCE: ONE OF DIOR'S SYMBOLS FOR GOOD LUCK
INSPIRED: DRESS COLLECTIONS AND FRAGRANCES

Another key symbol of superstition for Christian Dior can be found in the humble yet fragrant lily of the valley, which he was known to carry in his pocket. The flower is said to represent spring and is often celebrated in France on the first day of May, a tradition that the designer respected by gifting all employees of the fashion house with a sprig.

It's said that bouquets of lily of the valley were positioned around the salon on 12 February 1947 when the world was introduced to the New Look collection. A further nod to the floral species in his designs came in 1954 when Monsieur Dior dedicated his Muguet collection to the flower, with many of the gowns taking inspiration from the bell-shaped sepals. It's also reported that Dior would sew sprigs of lily of the valley into the hems of his designs.

Just two years later, Dior launched the fragrance Diorissimo, which they describe as "dramatic, extravagant and sophisticated", and famously features notes from the flower. Since then, Dior's association with lily of the valley has remained strong, with the image appearing in the form of embroidery, brooches and prints throughout the years. In 2013, Dior Maison launched the "New Lily of the Valley" tableware collection which paid homage to the bloom through a range of Limoges porcelain pieces.

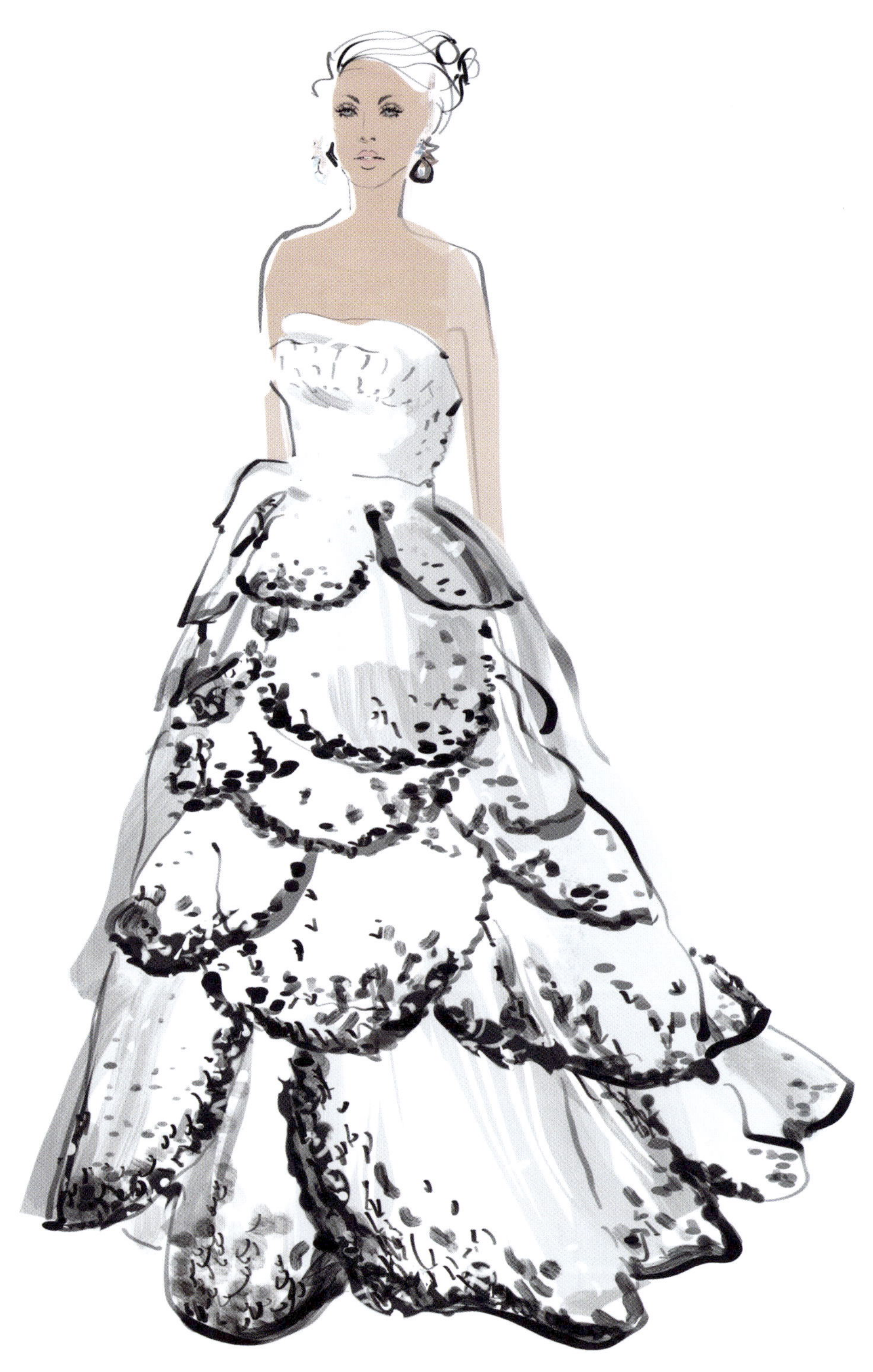

18

JUNON DRESS

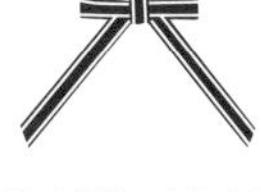

DATE: 1949

STYLE: STRAPLESS, LAYERED

MATERIALS: SILK, SEQUINS

Featuring a strapless cut with a tulle skirt, with countless sequins sewn into the gown with the help of esteemed embroiderer René Bégué, the "Junon" dress was an instant hit when it was introduced to the world as a part of Dior's autumn/winter 1949 haute couture collection. Dior took inspiration and the dress's name from Hera, wife of king of the gods Zeus, and looked to the peacock – her preferred creature – for the skirt's design.

Tulle petal-like shapes were layered atop each other with a sequin design that was compared to the peacock's distinct style of feathers. The gown has acted as a source of inspiration for a number of Dior's artistic directors since its initial debut, with John Galliano presenting his own rendition of the dress in 2010 and Maria Grazia Chiuri including her take, referred to as "the New Junon", as part of her first collection for the French fashion house in 2017. Kim Jones also released a top for Dior Men that closely referenced the Junon dress for his autumn/winter 2023 collection, while Dior ambassador Natalie Portman wore a recreation of the gown to a red-carpet event in 2023.

The Junon dress now resides in The Costume Institute at The Metropolitan Museum of Art in New York City.

19

PRINCESS MARGARET'S 21ST BIRTHDAY DRESS

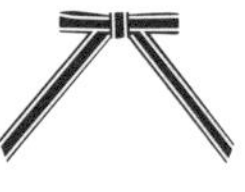

DATE: 1951
STYLE: OFF-THE-SHOULDER, LAYERED
FABRIC: SILK ORGANZA
SEEN: IN ONE OF THE MOST ICONIC PHOTOGRAPHS OF THE TWENTIETH CENTURY

"He loved the idea of British women in tweed and their ball gowns and he loved this idea of aristocracy and royalty," the V&A's fashion and textiles curator, Oriole Cullen, told the BBC in 2019 when remarking on Christian Dior's admiration for Britain.

Sparked after a trip across the Channel at 21 years old, Dior's affinity for the elegance of the British royal family would turn into a professional relationship when Princess Margaret paid a visit to one of the designer's salons during a trip to Paris in 1949. From then on, Dior became a firm favourite for the young princess and he of her (he described her as "a real fairy-tale princess, delicate, graceful, exquisite" in his 1950 autobiography). Dior, therefore, became an obvious choice to design a dress for her 21st birthday in 1951. The dress was crafted from silk organza in a soft cream colourway, adorned with pearls and sequins in a floral design across its seven-layer skirt. It was captured in a now-iconic image by royal photographer Cecil Beaton, which is often regarded as one of the most famous photographs of the twentieth century.

Princess Margaret, Countess of Snowdon, is said to have referred to the dress as her all-time favourite, and she remained a loyal Dior client throughout her life.

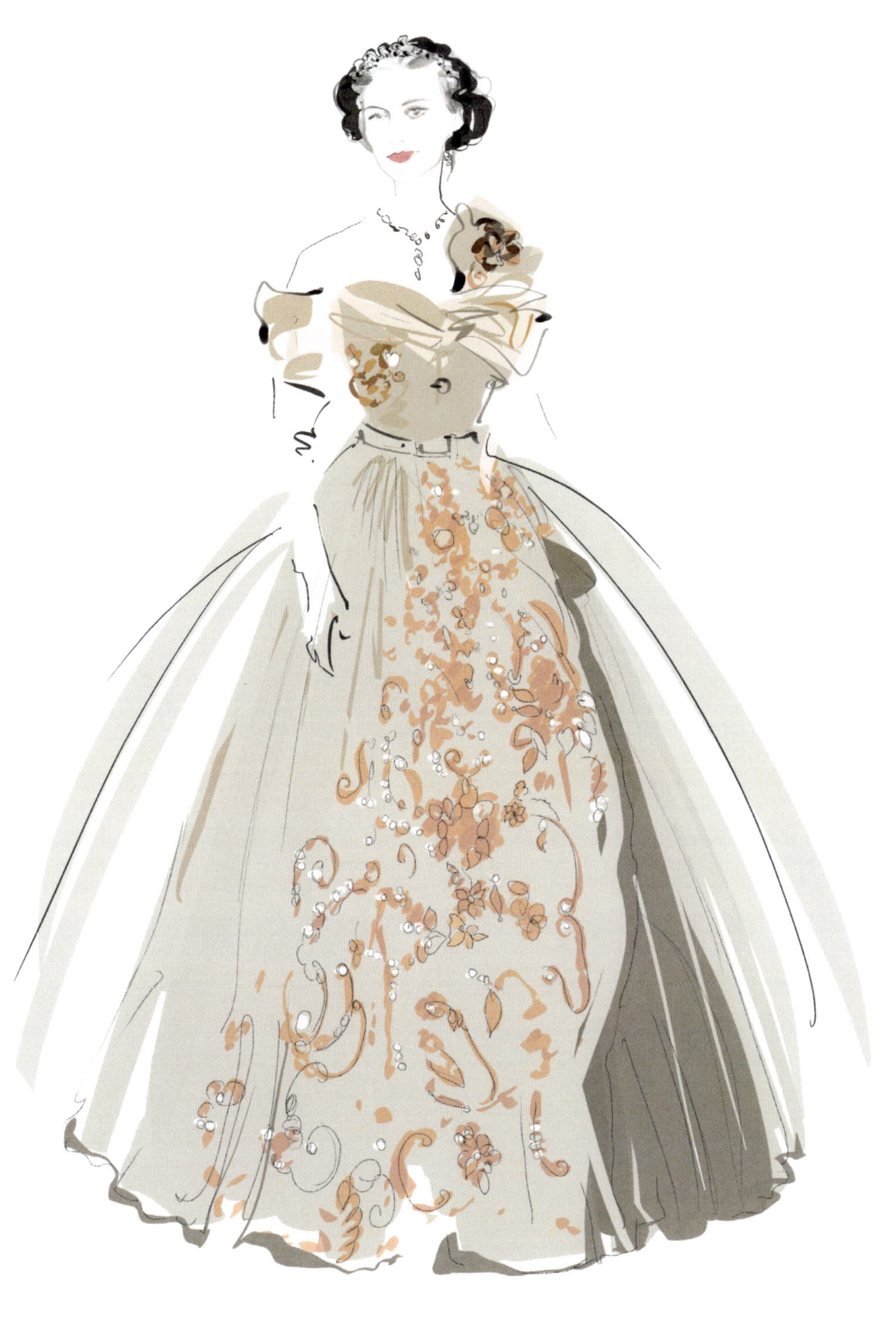

20

THE TULIP SILHOUETTE

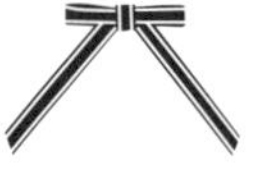

DATE: 1953

EMPHASIZED: A SHORTER HEM AND CINCHED WAIST

SYMBOLISM: DRAWN FROM FLORAL INSPIRATION IN BOTH CONSTRUCTION AND PRINTED FABRICS

It was 1953 when Christian Dior would steal almost as many headlines as his New Look collection had in 1947, this time by raising hemlines. One reviewer in the *Daily Express* remarked, "He brought back the short skirt", emphasizing Dior's change in direction from the New Look, which made him a key player in the fashion game of the era, partly due to his controversial take on the standard hem lengths of the time.

The Tulip collection offered a range of looks that prioritized padding and puff sleeves to exaggerate the upper half of the silhouette, a naturally slim waistline and a skirt that many compared to the stem of a flower. Florals were also a key source of inspiration for the collection's prints, which featured colourful blooms across silk organza gowns. Though there was plenty of colour, the collection also presented monochromatic looks that, some would argue, best demonstrate the distinct shape that Monsieur Dior had created for the season. These were often crafted from thick velvet or wool and shantung silk for their structural properties.

In 2010, John Galliano presented a fresh take on Dior's iconic 1953 collection with his autumn/winter 2010 haute couture season. Galliano used the tulip silhouette as the foundation for some of the season's key looks, putting his own spin on things in his signature extravagant fashion, proving the everlasting power of the original 1953 designs.

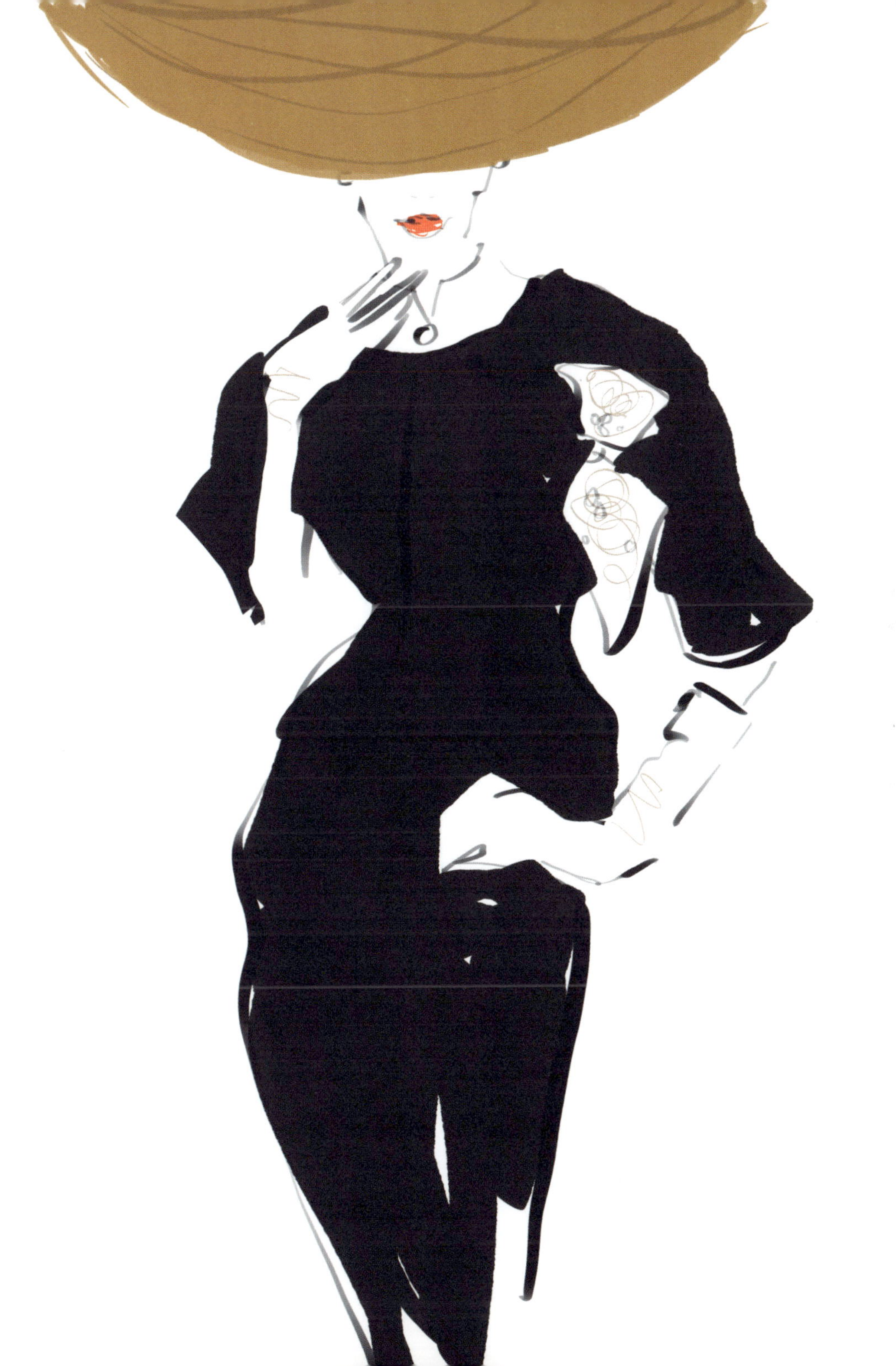

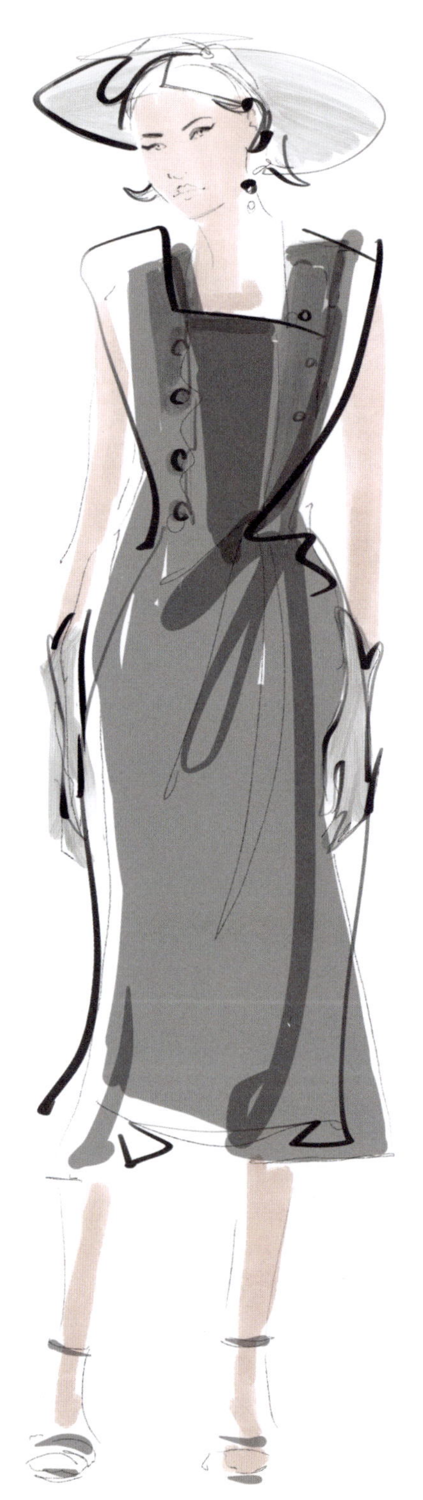

21

THE H-LINE

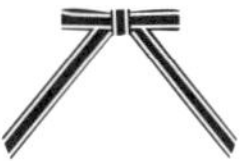

FEATURES: LONG SKIRTS, LOW WAISTS, HIGH NECKLINES
SIGNIFICANCE: MINIMALISM
INFLUENCED: MANY DIOR DESIGNERS, INCLUDING KIM JONES

In 1954, Christian Dior again got people talking with his H-Line collection, taking its name from the silhouette of high necklines and low waists, mimicking the shape of the letter "H". It was quickly referred to by some as the "runner bean" collection for its styles that minimized a woman's curves, which Dior's designs had previously celebrated.

The H-Line featured two key bodice looks that garnered much of the press's attention: the "Degas" and the "Tudor". The Degas offered an elongated torso and high neckline, with its name taken from French impressionist Edgar Degas (1834–1917), famous for his paintings of young ballerinas. The Tudor would push the wearer's bust high above the neckline, a look often associated with the historical period of its name.

Many see this collection as marking a new era for fashion, moving away from the excesses seen in previous years and towards a simplified approach: "A new woman is born … 1954's woman has straight shoulders, a high bust, trim hips and a slim but unexaggerated waist. She is a woman of her time. Her clothes are sober and supple, liberated from useless detail," *Vogue* claimed at the time. The impact of the H-Line can still be felt in both the wider fashion world and within the walls of Dior. Kim Jones proved this with his Dior Men autumn/winter 2025 season, referred to as "a subtle re-reading" of the H-Line collection from 1954, with square necklines and an emphasis on simplicity, just as the original boasted.

22

THE A-LINE

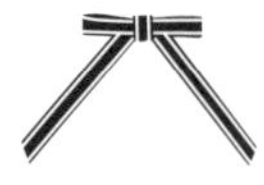

DATE: 1955

KEY LOOKS: COATS, DRESSES AND SKIRTS

LEGACY: CREDITED FOR INFLUENCING FASHION AROUND THE WORLD

In 1955, Christian Dior presented another silhouette that would change the fashion world forever. The A-line cut was defined by narrow shoulders and a flared skirt with a waistline that sat low on the hips, essentially creating a shape that could resemble the letter "A". Dresses, coats and suits took on this new shape and inspired comments referring to it as the "most wanted silhouette in Paris" by *Vogue* at the time. Key looks from the collection included a double-breasted tunic jacket that was designed to be worn over a corresponding dress to allow for optimal versatility between day- and eveningwear.

The collection also featured plenty of gowns fit for a ball. "The simplicity of the lines of the evening dresses is admirably matched by the enrichment they bring. Sumptuous but discreet, they take their theme from the women of the Indies and the Trianon," read the official press release. Dresses from the collection were among the favourites of a number of stars of the day, including actress Olivia de Havilland, who wore a suit from the line when she married *Paris Match* editor Pierre Galante in 1955.

The A-line cut remains a key silhouette throughout the fashion world and is often noted in fashion encyclopaedias across the globe.

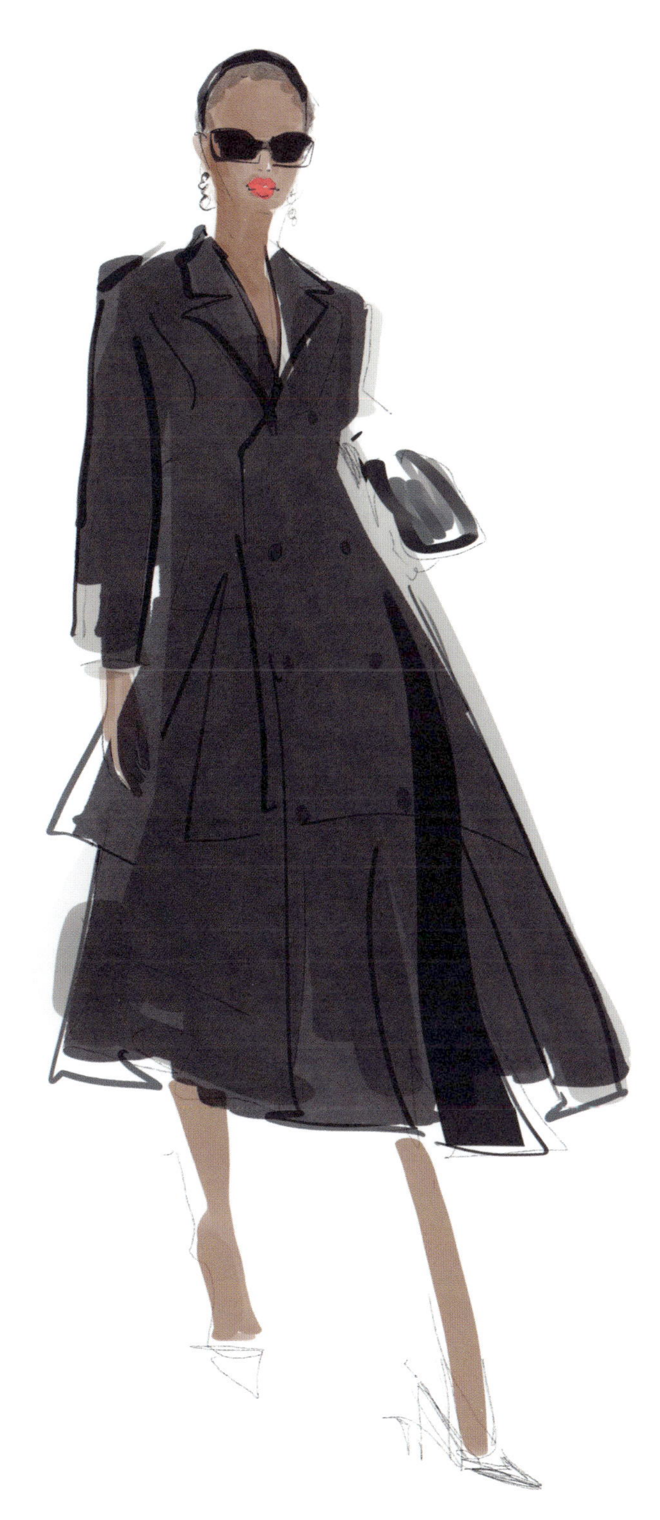

23

THE Y-LINE

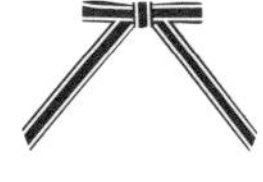

DATE: 1955

STYLE: HEAVY UPPER WITH SLIM BODY

***VOGUE* DESCRIBED AS**: "BULK AGAINST SLIMNESS"

Following the A-line collection earlier in the year, Dior launched the Y collection for the Autumn/Winter 1955 season. Some drew similarities to the Tulip collection, which Dior had released a few years earlier, while others remarked that the Y-line took the A-line and flipped it upside down. Both the Tulip and Y-line put a strong emphasis on the collars and upper half of the silhouette, often paired with a narrow skirt. *Vogue* called the collection "Bulk against slimness" in its September 1955 issue.

One of the ways in which Dior added weight to the collars and shoulders was by adding padding, stoles or even bolero jackets crafted from materials like wool herringbone or, as one report in *Vogue* states, beaver fur lining. The collection which followed was for Spring/Summer 1956 and was entitled Arrow, offering silhouettes which took influence from the Y line but notably offered waistlines that were lifted even further. The Y line would end up being one of the final collections released before Christian's untimely death in 1957, further cementing its status as a pivotal collection in the history of the maison.

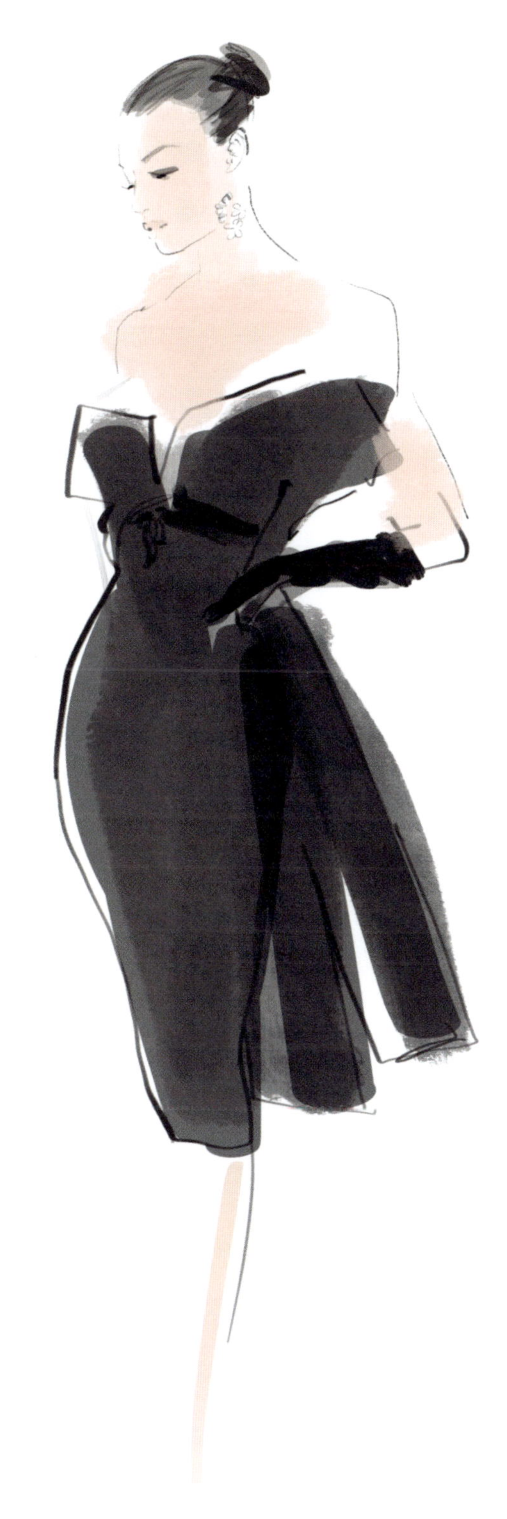

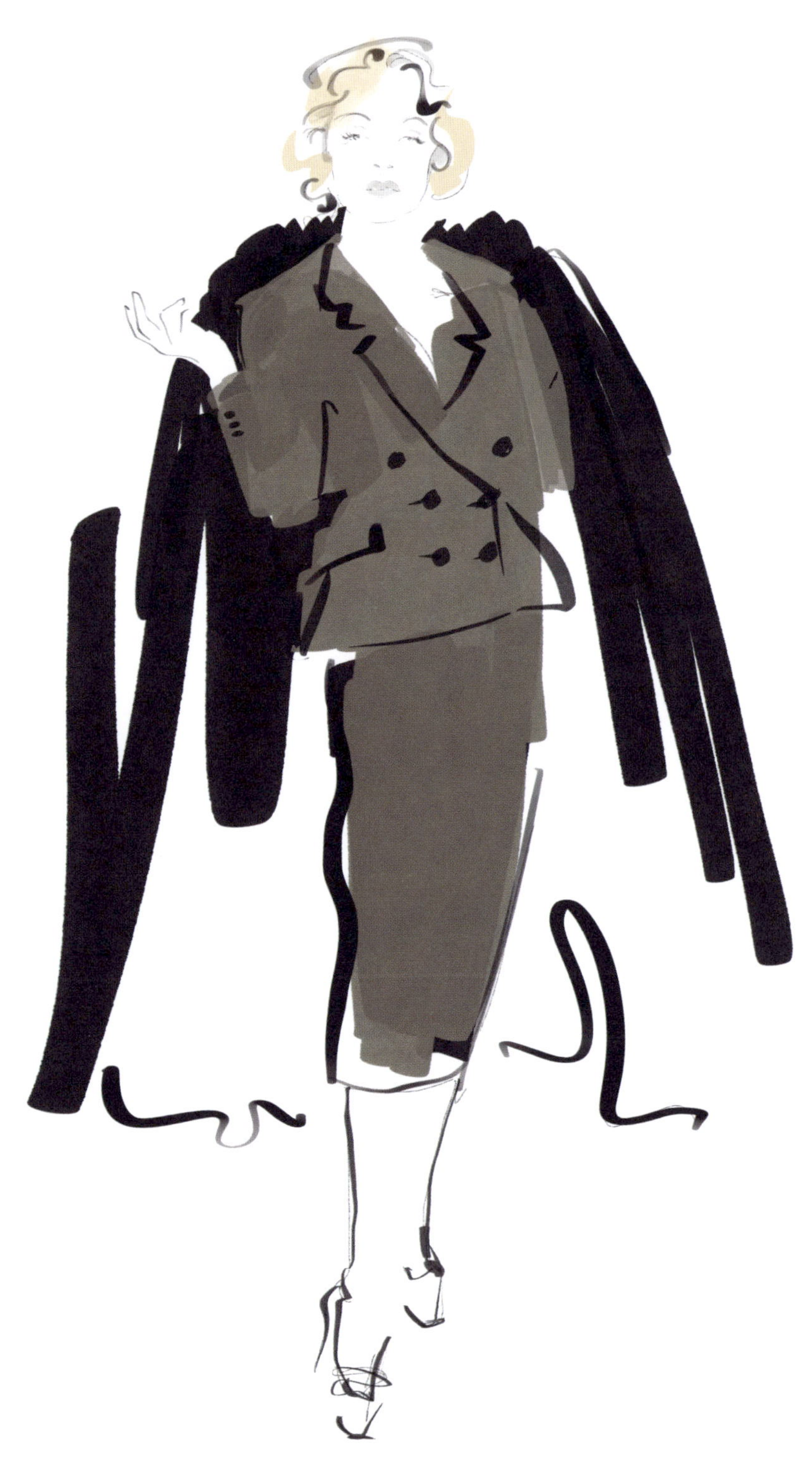

24

MARLENE DIETRICH

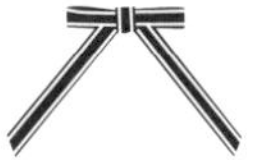

RELATIONSHIP: FRIEND AND FREQUENT WEARER OF DIOR
CEMENTED: THE BRAND'S LINKS TO HOLLYWOOD GLAMOUR
LEGACY: CONTEMPORARY COLLECTIONS HAVE BEEN BASED ON DIETRICH'S FAVOURITE PIECES AND STYLES

Marlene Dietrich can easily be hailed as one of the most important female actors of the twentieth century and her distinct approach to fashion played an important role in the public's fascination with the star. Dietrich and Dior crossed paths for the first time in the late 1940s when introduced by a mutual friend, French poet and playwright Jean Cocteau, and it's reported the pair became fast friends.

Dietrich's admiration for Dior became evident when, in 1949, she demanded to be dressed only in Dior's designs for her role in Alfred Hitchcock's 1950 film, *Stage Fright* ("No Dior, no Dietrich," she's said to have proclaimed during contract negotiations). But it wasn't just Dietrich being inspired by Dior; it's rumoured that the designer himself also looked to Dietrich for inspiration.

"Dior copied her, not the other way round," her grandson, Peter Riva, told journalist Natasha Fraser-Cavassoni in her 2014 book, *Monsieur Dior: Once Upon a Time*. "It was always a close cooperation," he added.

Marlene Dietrich would continue to wear Dior throughout her career and remained a loyal fan until her death in 1992. Fast forward to 2024 and it would be proven that Dietrich's influence on Dior was still felt within the walls of the fashion house with the autumn/winter 2024 collection being based on the American-German actor, with Maria Grazia Chiuri notably reimagining one of Dietrich's favourite styles, the "Acacia" jacket, for the modern woman.

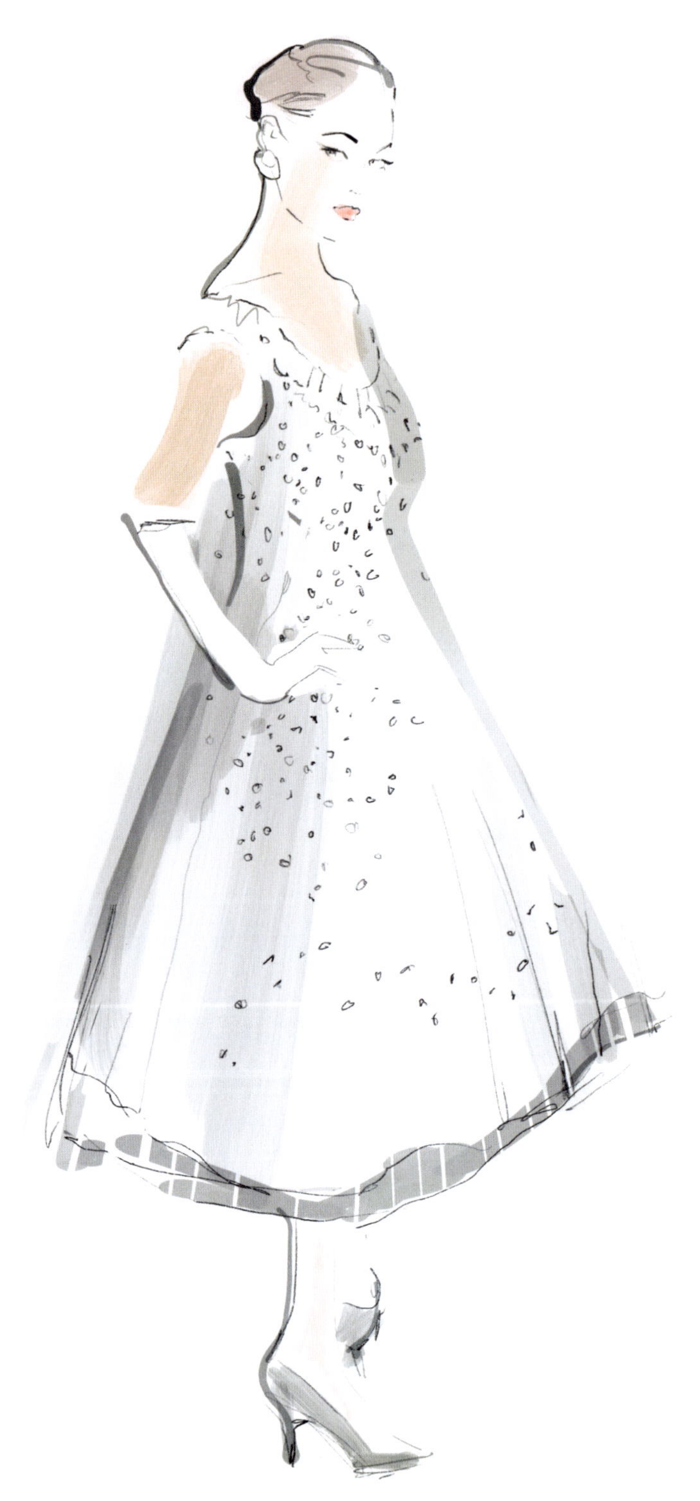

25

SUMMER TRAPÈZE DRESS

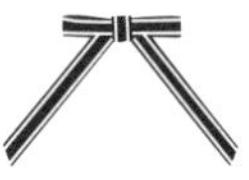

DATE: 1958

CREATED BY: YVES SAINT LAURENT

IMPACT: INTRODUCED A NEW SILHOUETTE TO THE WORLD OF FASHION

Following the untimely death from a heart attack of Christian Dior in 1957, a 21-year-old designer who went by the name Yves Saint Laurent would take up the reins as head designer for the Dior brand. The young designer's talents would immediately shine bright with his first offering for the label, the spring/summer 1958 collection. Among the looks that captivated the audiences was the "L'Eléphant Blanc" dress, a sleeveless style that caught the light with its intricate Rocailles beaded embroidery over a tulle top layer, with an intricate corset and stiff horsehair construction hidden underneath to achieve the distinct shape.

But beyond the shimmering beadwork, the dress also presented a whole new silhouette to the fashion world – the "Trapèze". Following the precedent that Christian Dior had set with his "H", "A" and "Y" lines, Saint Laurent likely knew he had to introduce a new shape to ensure the Dior name remained synonymous with innovation even with a new figure at the helm. The Trapèze silhouette, defined by its slim shoulders, waist-less silhouette and swinging skirt, was widely hailed a success by fashion critics of the time and would go on to influence the wider fashion world for decades to come, including playing a key role in the decade-defining look of the 1960s.

26

EAU SAUVAGE FRAGRANCE

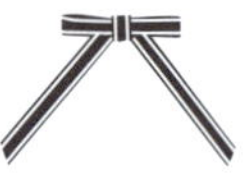

DATE: 1966

CREATED BY: CHRISTIAN DIOR / EDMOND ROUDNITSKA

FRAGRANCE: BERGAMOT, HEDIONE AND LAVENDER

After years of men adopting Dior's Eau Fraîche fragrance due to its subtle fragrance and ungendered adverts, Dior released its first fragrances especially made for men. Dior brought in the talents of French perfumer and writer Edmond Roudnitska, who had previously worked on the brand's Diorissimo fragrance in 1955.

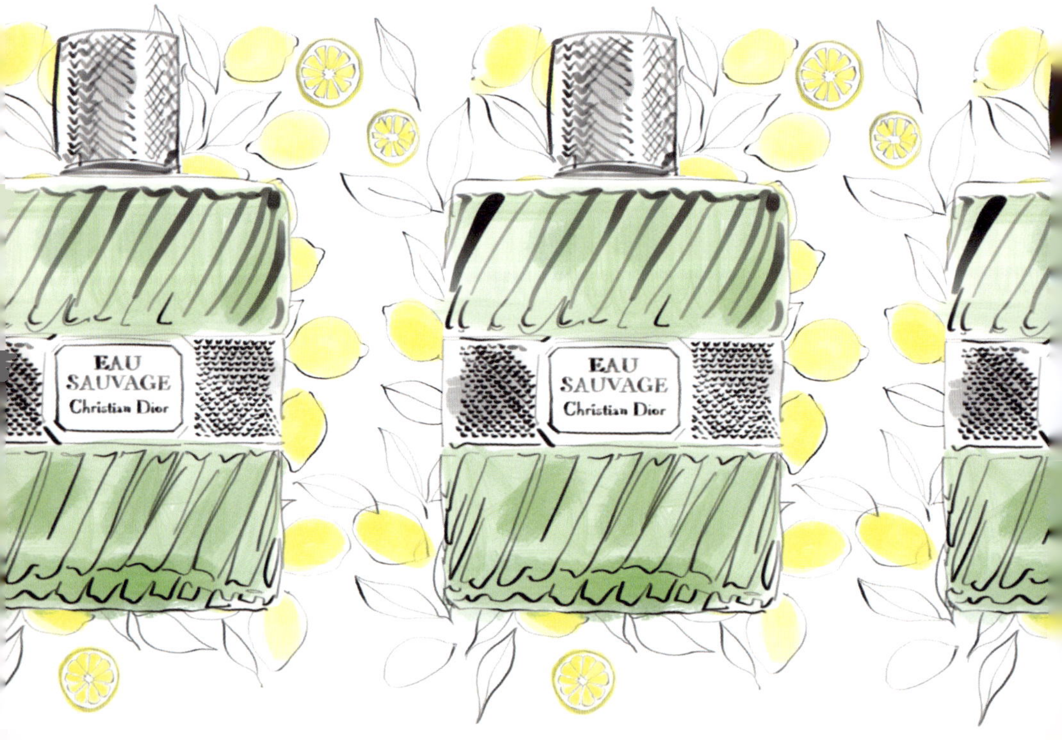

The name is rumoured to come from Australia-born designer and fashion publicist Percy Savage, who was a close friend of Christian Dior. The story behind the perfume is not dissimilar to that of the naming of Miss Dior, as it's reported that Mr Savage arrived to see Dior as the designer was looking for a name for the fragrance and he considered this to be a sign (Miss Dior came about as Dior's sister Catherine arrived as he was contemplating the name for the fragrance and Dior's muse and confidante Mitzah Bricard proclaimed, "Ah, here's Miss Dior!").

Many credit a large portion of Eau Sauvage's success to its incorporation of an innovative ingredient by the name of hedione (derived from the Greek word for pleasure). This compound is said to have transformed the fragrance world due to its ability to stimulate the amygdala and hippocampus areas of the brain, which are often associated with emotional and hormonal responses. It's due to this that many theorize hedione's ability to act as something of an aphrodisiac. Actor Steve McQueen was known to wear Eau Sauvage during the filming of many of his Hollywood hits, while more recently Antonio Banderas is a notable fan of the fragrance.

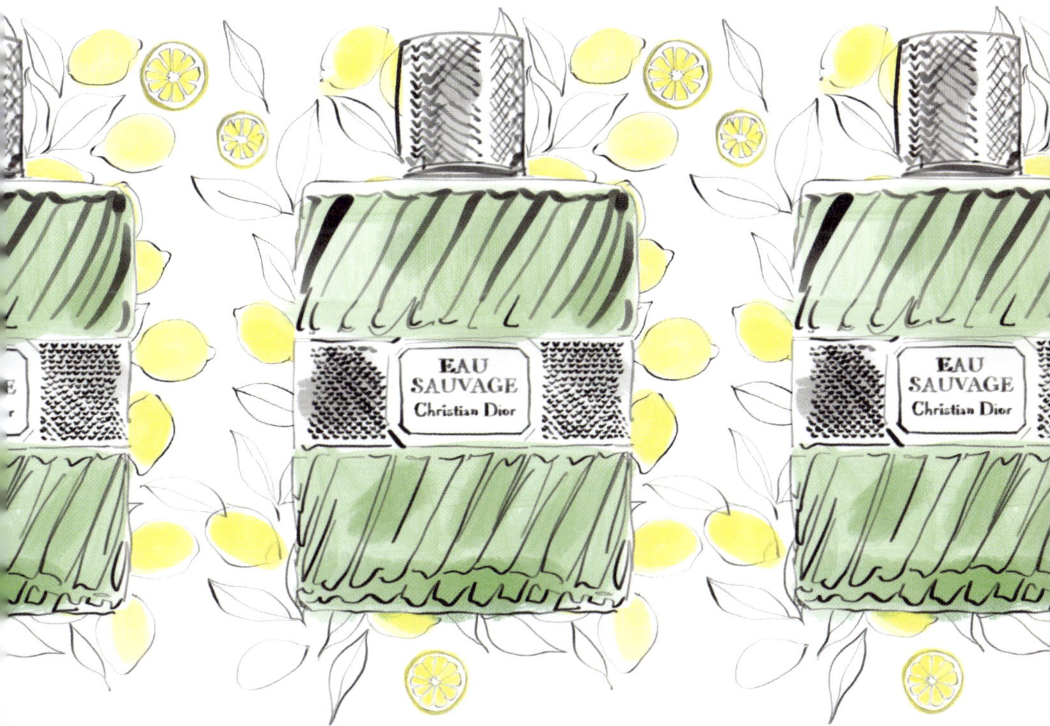

27

ROUGE DIOR

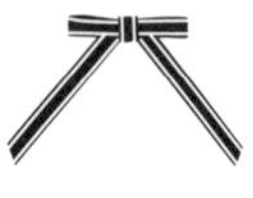

DATE: 1953

IMPACT: BROADENED THE HOUSE'S REACH TO MORE WOMEN

WORN BY: GRACE KELLY, MARLENE DIETRICH, JOSEPHINE BAKER

The Dior name first entered the cosmetics arena in 1949 when a lipstick was released as a limited-edition (only 350 lipsticks were made) gift with purchase for shoppers at the prestigious Avenue Montaigne boutique around the Christmas season. But it would be in the early 1950s, just a few years after the world was introduced to the New Look, when Rouge Dior would become a favourite for the world's most fashion-forward women alongside Hollywood's hottest names of the era, including Grace Kelly, Marlene Dietrich and Josephine Baker. Two years later, Parfums Christian Dior would launch its first lipstick boxed sets, offering an impressive 22 unique shade options. Much like Dior dresses, the shades for these lipsticks were said to have been inspired by Christian Dior's favourite flowers.

Beyond the striking shades, Dior's approach to lipstick was far ahead of its time in the 1950s. Two separate types of lipstick were created: one referred to as "*objet d'art*", designed to be a statement piece to live on the counter of your vanity at home, and another to be your on-the-go option, designed to easily pop in your handbag. But the real innovation came in the fact that both were refillable. Once your tube was running low, simply head to your local Dior cosmetics counter to replenish. Dior lipsticks continue to be adored for their striking pigmentation and long-lasting wear by make-up lovers across the world.

As a 1959 Dior marketing campaign would say: "All women can't wear Dior, but they all can wear Dior's lipsticks".

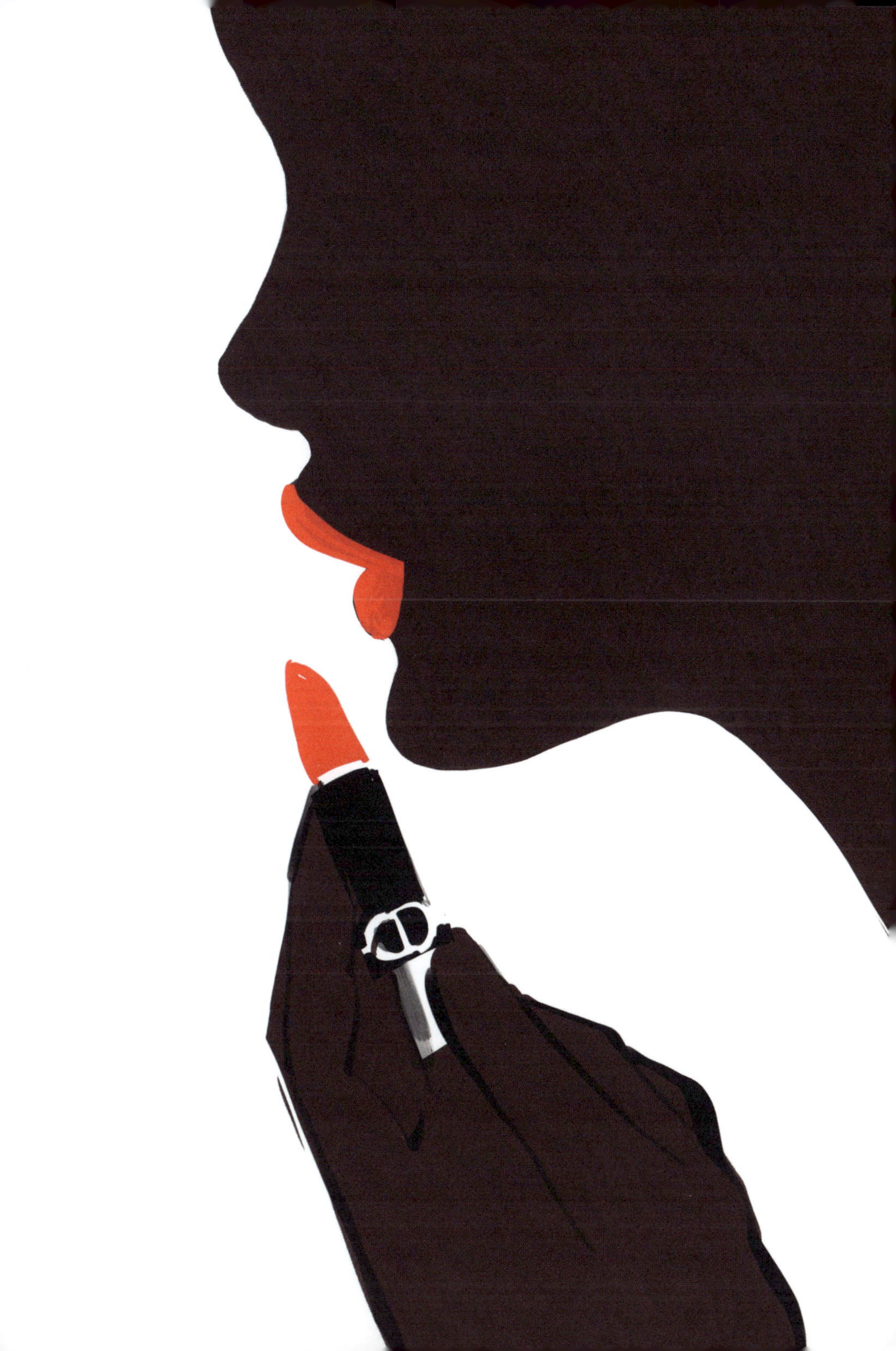

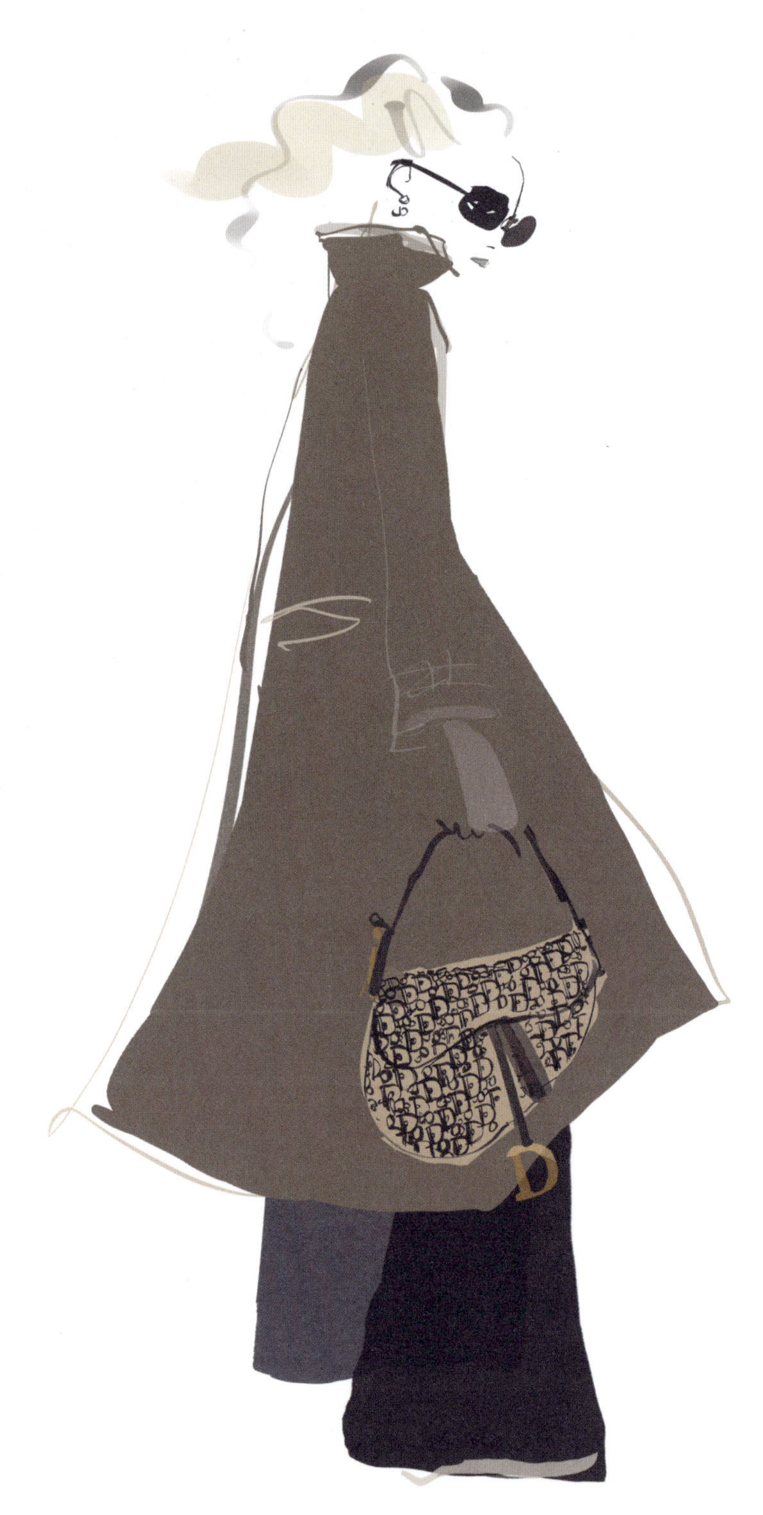

28

DIOR SADDLE BAG

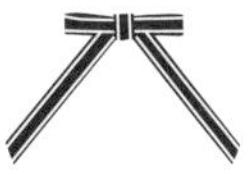

DATE: 2000

MATERIALS: GRAIN LEATHER STRAP, VARIOUS MATERIALS INCLUDING PATTERNED CANVAS, EMBOSSED CALFSKIN AND EMBROIDERED DENIM

WORN BY: SARAH JESSICA PARKER, RIHANNA, BELLA HADID

Since John Galliano (1960–) brought us the Dior Saddle Bag as a part of his spring/summer 2000 collection, the "Saddle Bag" has become a key trademark style for the French fashion house. This popularity can be partly attributed to its frequent appearances on the arms of some of the top It girls of the 00s – from *The O.C.*'s Mischa Barton to Paris Hilton to Sarah Jessica Parker in *Sex and the City*.

The handbag, defined by its equestrian-influenced shape that mimics that of a jockey's saddle, was everywhere throughout the early- to mid-00s before many of its fans retired it to the back of their wardrobes towards the latter half of the decade. But in 2018, the sculpted accessory would again become a fashion hit when it appeared on the catwalk once more. The new iterations of the Saddle Bag included timeless grain leather constructions alongside Dior's Oblique pattern on canvas with both the classic shoulder bag style and a miniature version available.

29

ELIZABETH TAYLOR

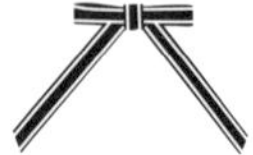

IMPACT: WORE DIOR GOWNS TO MULTIPLE HOLLYWOOD RED CARPET EVENTS
SIGNIFICANCE: CONSIDERED HER OSCARS DRESS A LUCKY CHARM AND KEPT IT FOR YEARS AFTER
LEGACY: BOOSTED DIOR'S IMAGE AS A BRAND FOR A-LIST STARS

The Dior name has always been on the tips of the tongues of plenty of A-listers, especially when it comes to their red-carpet looks.

In 1961, Elizabeth Taylor was nominated for the Oscar for Best Actress for her role as a socialite in *Butterfield 8* and knew that only a Dior dress would do for the occasion. Marc Bohan had only just joined Dior, but hit the ground running with his spring/summer 1961 Dior haute couture collection, which featured Taylor's sleeveless look with embroidered bubble skirt and floral belt piece.

The gown is said to have remained in Taylor's closet for decades following the event and was regarded as somewhat of a good-luck charm for her (she won the award that night after being nominated and losing in the same category on five previous occasions).

Elizabeth Taylor would make headlines in Dior again that year when, while attending a film festival in Moscow, she would run into a fellow attendee in an almost-identical dress. The story goes that Marc Bohan had created the dress specially for Taylor but, on spotting it, the Italian actress and model Gina Lollobrigida had fallen in love with the design and orchestrated a copy to be made for her behind Bohan's back, not knowing that Taylor would be wearing the dress to the same event. Despite this episode, Taylor would continue to be a loyal fan of Dior throughout her life until her passing in 2011.

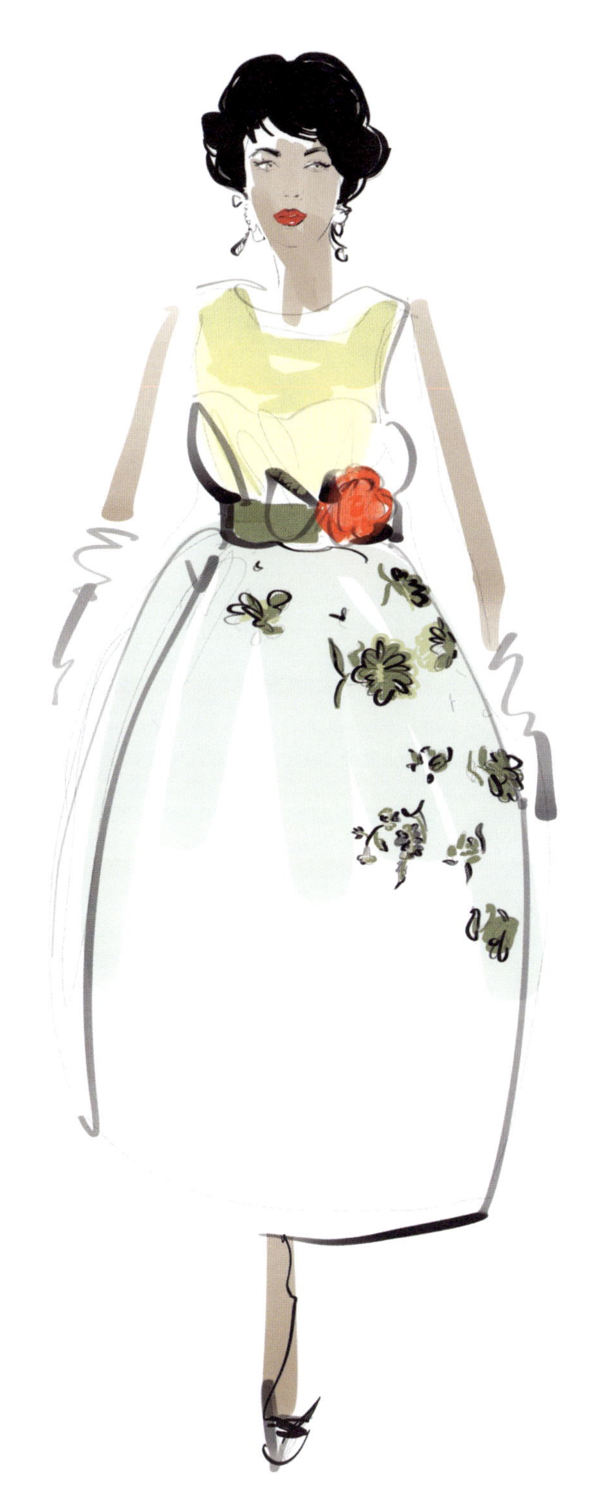

30

J'ADORE

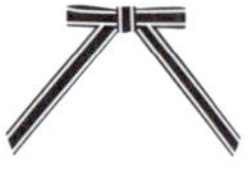

DATE: 1999

CREATED BY: CALICE BECKER

FRAGRANCE: JASMINE, LILY OF THE VALLEY, MANDARIN ORANGE AND MELON

For many, J'Adore is so much more than simply a fragrance. Since its launch in 1999, it has become one of Dior's most iconic creations, thanks in part to its star-studded, ethereal advertisements.

The talents of French master perfumer Calice Becker, who completed her training at Givaudan Academy in Grasse, were called upon to create a scent that mimicked "what solid gold would smell like if it had a scent", according to the notes of the 2023 *Dior J'Adore* exhibition at Beaux-arts de Paris. Though some remark on the formula changing over the years, the original was said to have 80 ingredients with notes that include fresh jasmine, lily of the valley, mandarin orange and melon. The bottle – adorned with gold-tone rings forming a "necklace" leading from the body to the glass cap – was noted by designer Hervé Van der Straeten to have been influenced by John Galliano's take on the female silhouette, and amphoras from Ancient Greece.

Upon its original release, supermodel Carmen Kass starred in the now-iconic advertisements for the fragrance, which saw her wading through a pool of gold liquid. By 2004, Charlize Theron had become the face of the fragrance, where she stayed for an impressive 20 years before Rihanna took the role in 2024, with a campaign showing her dressing in a shimmering gold gown and stacked necklace before walking through Versailles. "Nowhere else in the world could you be surrounded by as much gold as Versailles. It is a dream in gold!" she told *Vogue*.

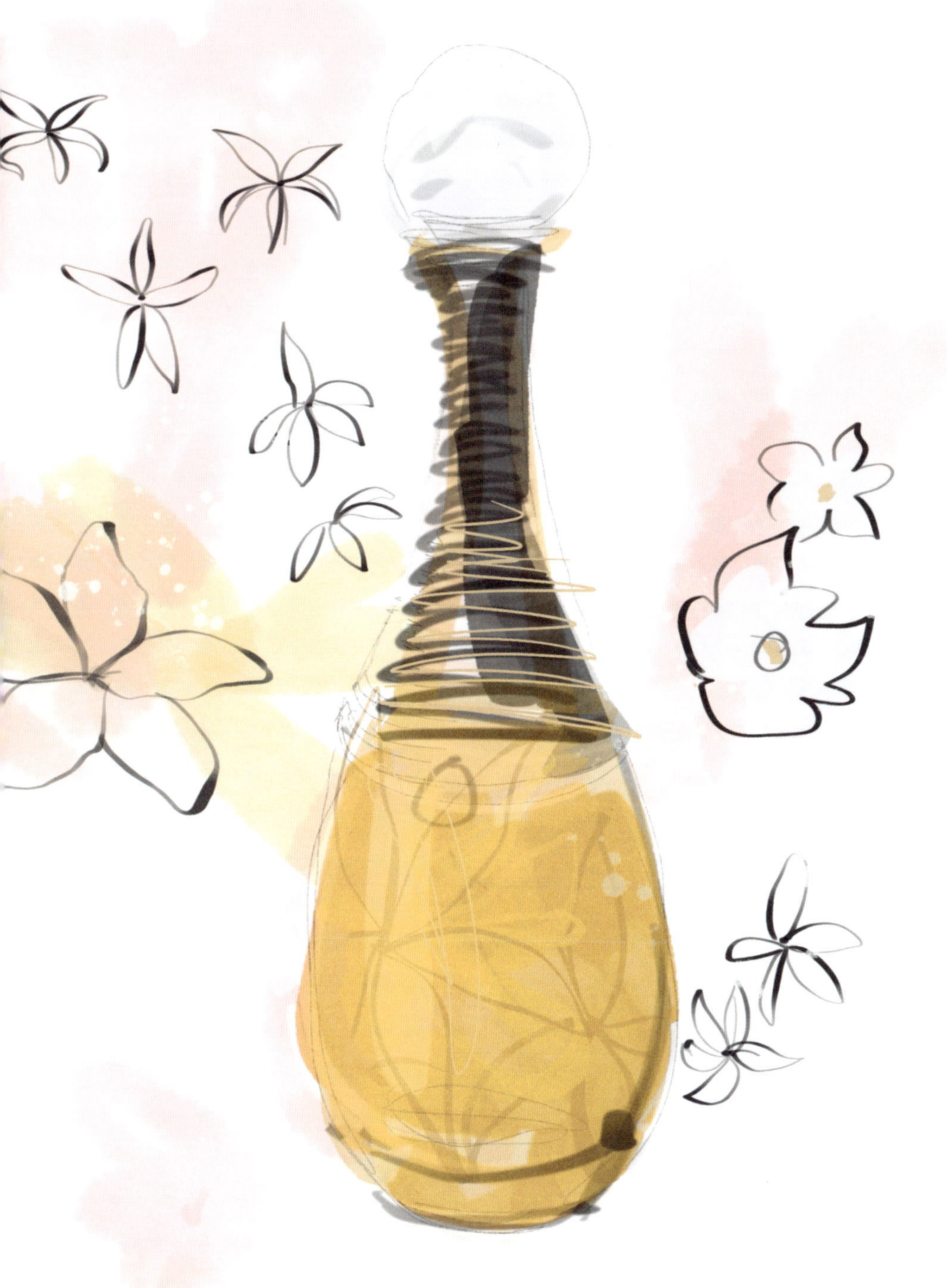

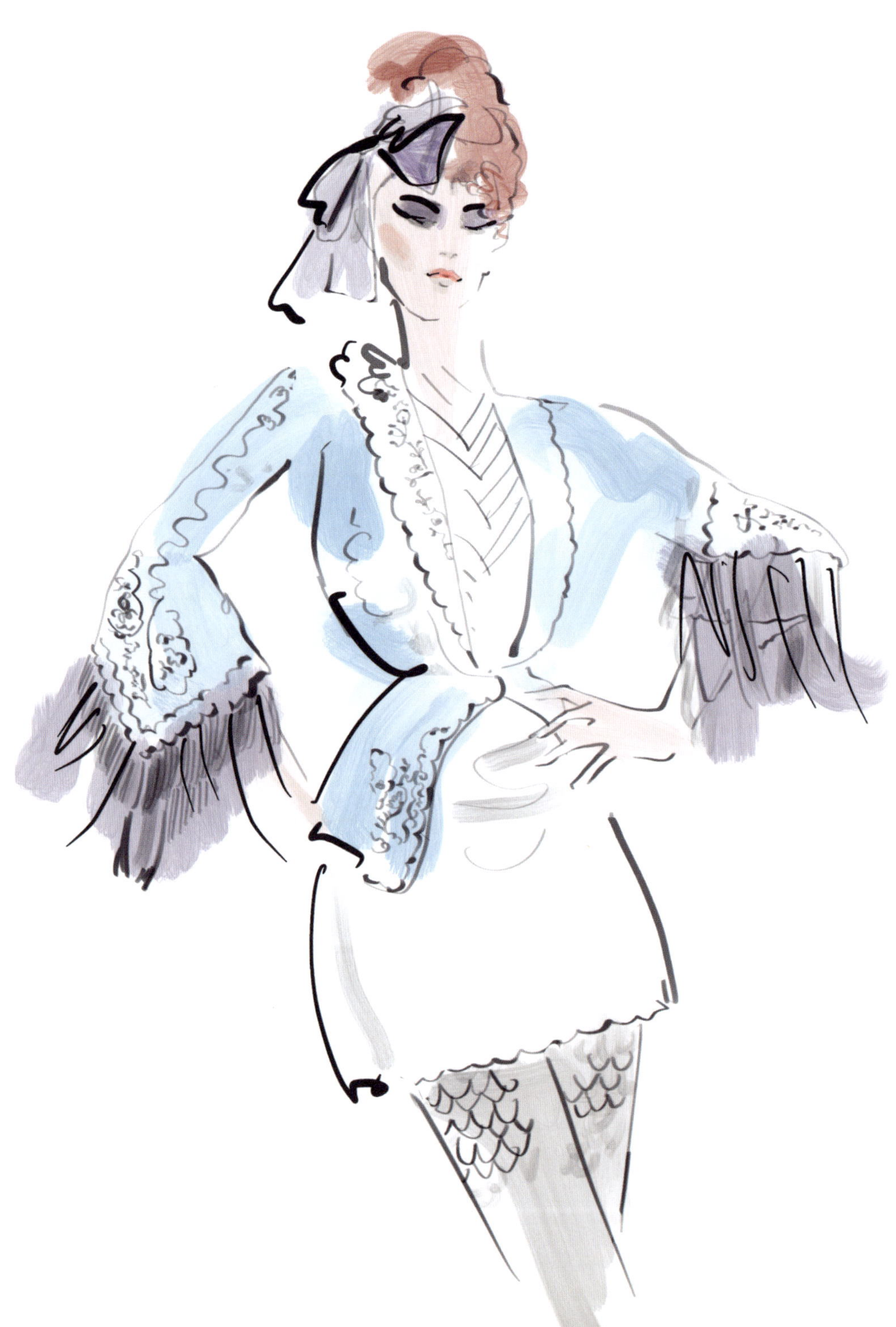

31

LA BELLE ÉPOQUE

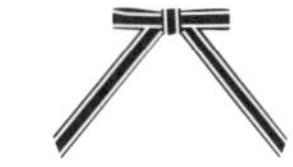

DATE: 1871–1914

AESTHETIC: FLOUNCES, CORSETRY, BOWS, CINCHED WAISTS

INSPIRED: STRUCTURED DRESSES AND SILHOUETTES

"I thank heaven I lived in Paris in the last years of the Belle Époque. They marked me for life. My memory holds a picture of a time full of happiness, exuberance and peace in which everything was directed toward the art of living," Christian Dior shared in his memoir, *Dior by Dior*, published in 1956.

The Frenchman's adoration for this period can be seen in almost every corner of his work, from the structured cuts of his New Look collection drawing comparisons to the sculpted silhouettes at the end of the nineteenth century to the interiors of 30 Avenue Montaigne, which displayed panelling reminiscent of the Petit Trianon at Versailles, alongside a model of the château's Temple of Love, which acted as a cosmetics stand. And the love for this period would continue until his final designs. One of the best examples can be found in the "Du Barry" dress from his final collection of 1957. The dress, which now resides in the archives of the Met's Costume Institute, took its name from King Louis XV's mistress, Jeanne Bécu, Comtesse du Barry, and features a strapless cut with structured dome skirt and coquettish bows reminiscent of the period from which it takes its inspiration. The iconic Belle Époque continues to provide bountiful inspiration for the helms of the fashion house, being notably one of John Galliano's preferred sources, as demonstrated starkly in his autumn/winter 1997 collection, which many recall for its corset cuts and billowing skirts.

32

THE SLIM LOOK

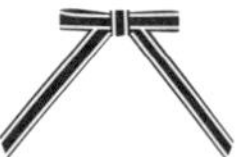

CREATED BY: MARC BOHAN
FEATURES: SLEEK, SIMPLIFIED SILHOUETTES
WORN BY: JACKIE KENNEDY AND OLIVIA DE HAVILLAND

In 1961, a press release from Dior referred to its latest collection, stating, "The silhouette is supple, slim, the shoulders are natural, the waist fluid, the hips are very flat." This fresh approach was introduced by Marc Bohan, newly appointed artistic director of the fashion house following a short stint by Yves Saint Laurent, who shifted into the role after Christian Dior's sudden passing in 1957. Bohan's spring/summer 1961 collection is said to have been inspired by the Flapper look of the 1920s, pared back in comparison to much of Christian's designs throughout the 50s, which were renowned for their structural constructions, often playing with exaggerated proportions. The key takeaway from this season was referred to as "the slim look", the simplified shape that would quickly go on to help define the look of the decade.

Some of the era's top style stars would rush to get their hands on certain pieces from the collection, including First Lady Jackie Kennedy, who wore the *Vie en Rose* coat during a trip to Venezuela in December 1961. Other pieces from the collection can be seen in the 1962 film, *Light in the Piazza*, where Olivia de Havilland's character dons a number of looks, including a two-piece outfit comprised of double-breasted jacket and pleated skirt that sat just above the knee.

Dior paid homage to Bohan's iconic collection with its spring/summer 2022 collection, wherein former artistic director Maria Grazia Chiuri recreated many of the original looks while refreshing things with an ultra-modern colour palette and contemporary details.

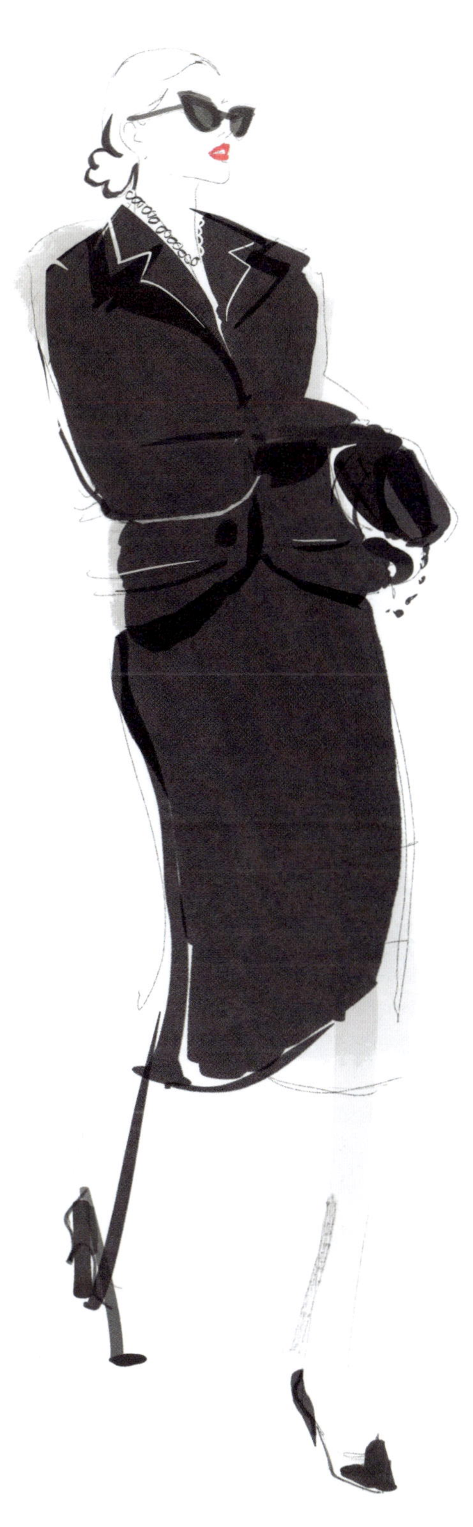

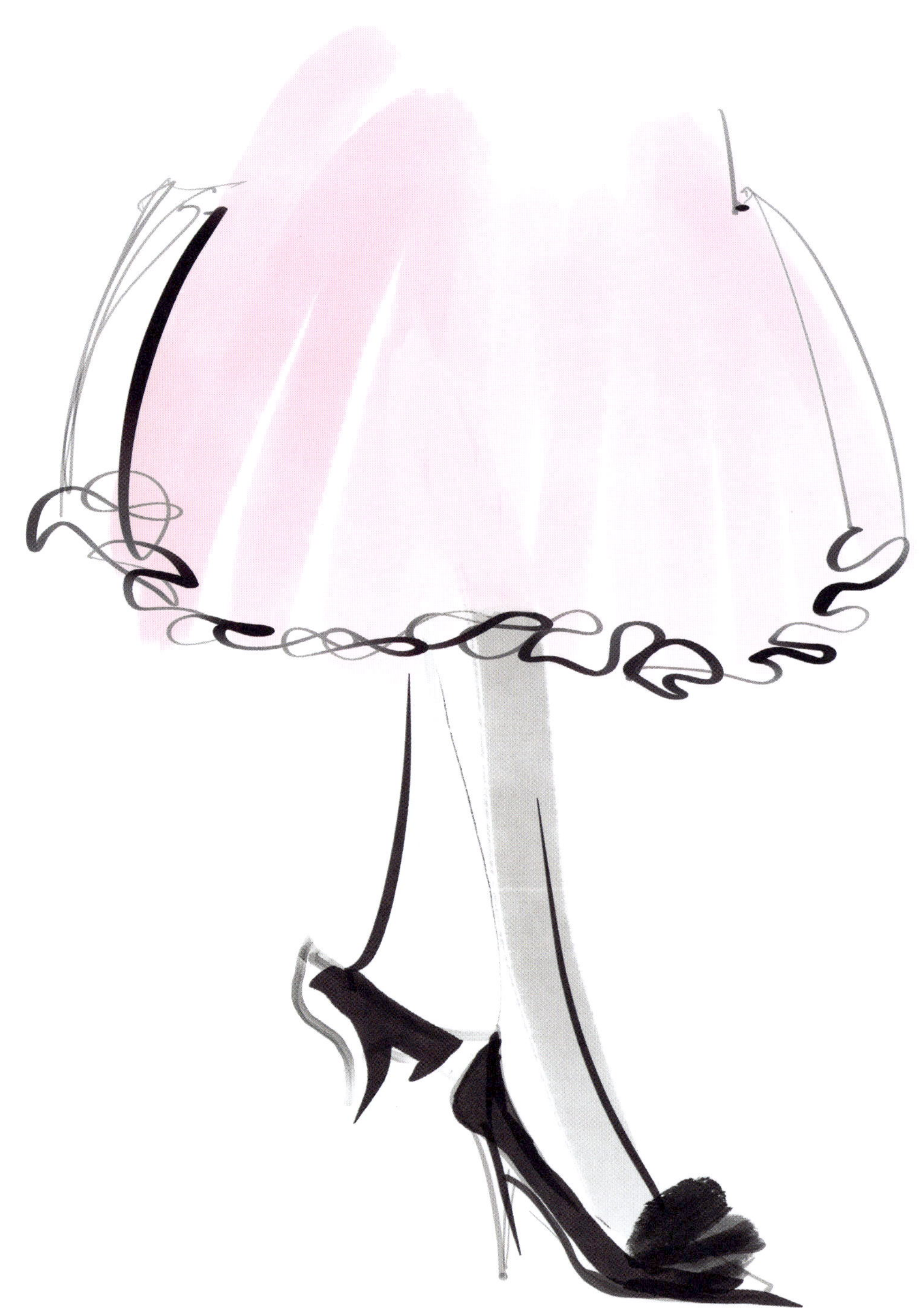

33

ROGER VIVIER

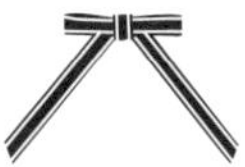

RELATIONSHIP: FRIEND AND COLLABORATOR
DESIGNED FOR DIOR: 1953–1963
SIGNATURES: STILETTO HEEL, BEADING

Roger Vivier was another key figure who played an important role in cementing Dior's philosophy of creating head-to-toe looks for fashion-forward women across the globe. Joining forces with the French fashion house in 1953, Vivier quickly drew attention to Dior's footwear output with his designs inspired by sculpture and architecture which included early versions of the stiletto style referred to at the time as the "needle heel". Vivier's designs were also known for their intricate beading and embellishments that perfectly complemented Dior's gowns.

His time with Dior helped Vivier become known as one of the most innovative footwear designers of the day, often pushing boundaries with unexpected approaches like using heavily fragranced leather in his designs (the fragrances chosen were Dior perfumes, of course). Though Vivier left Dior in 1963 to create his namesake label, he continues to be an influence across the House of Dior, notably in Maria Grazia Chiuri's 2022 footwear designs which looked to Vivier's archival designs to create reinterpretations of his embroidery work across modern silhouettes.

Vivier's designs have also inspired a number of exhibitions around the world, among them the *Virgule, etc. In the Footsteps of Roger Vivier* exhibition at the Palais de Tokyo in Paris, 2013, and have also featured heavily in many Dior exhibitions, including the record-breaking *Christian Dior: Designer of Dreams* at London's V&A in 2019. A total of almost 595,000 people visited the exhibition in seven months.

34

GIANFRANCO FERRÉ'S WHITE SHIRTS

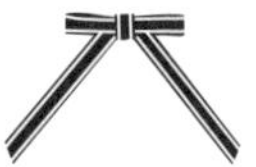

DATE: 1989–1996
SIGNIFICANCE: BROUGHT AN ITALIAN FLAIR AND ARCHITECTURAL INSPIRATIONS TO HIS DESIGNS
IMPACT: THE REINVENTED WHITE SHIRT BECAME HIS LEGACY AT DIOR

The era of Gianfranco Ferré at Dior is usually remembered for his dedication to elaborate designs and his over-the-top Italian attitude, so in a way the fact that his greatest legacy at the House of Dior would be something as simple as the white dress shirt may come as a surprise.

Ferré joined Dior in 1989 as the first artistic director to come from outside Paris (something that understandably caused a bit of a stir for the French fashion house at the time), but he quickly found his feet with his architectural-inspired designs and distinctive reinterpretations of a garment hung in countless wardrobes around the world, the white button-down shirt. In almost every one of his Dior collections, Ferré offered a new take on the shirt's style – playing with proportions and materials to create distinctive pieces that would go down in history as examples of the boundless ways in which, with true talent, a designer can put their stamp on the world.

The white shirts designed by Ferré would go on to inspire *The White Shirt According to Me*, an exhibition showcasing 27 styles from Ferré's archive spanning between 1989 and 1997. The exhibition would find its first home in the designer's home country of Italy, at the Prato Textile Museum, before travelling to the Phoenix Art Museum for its American debut.

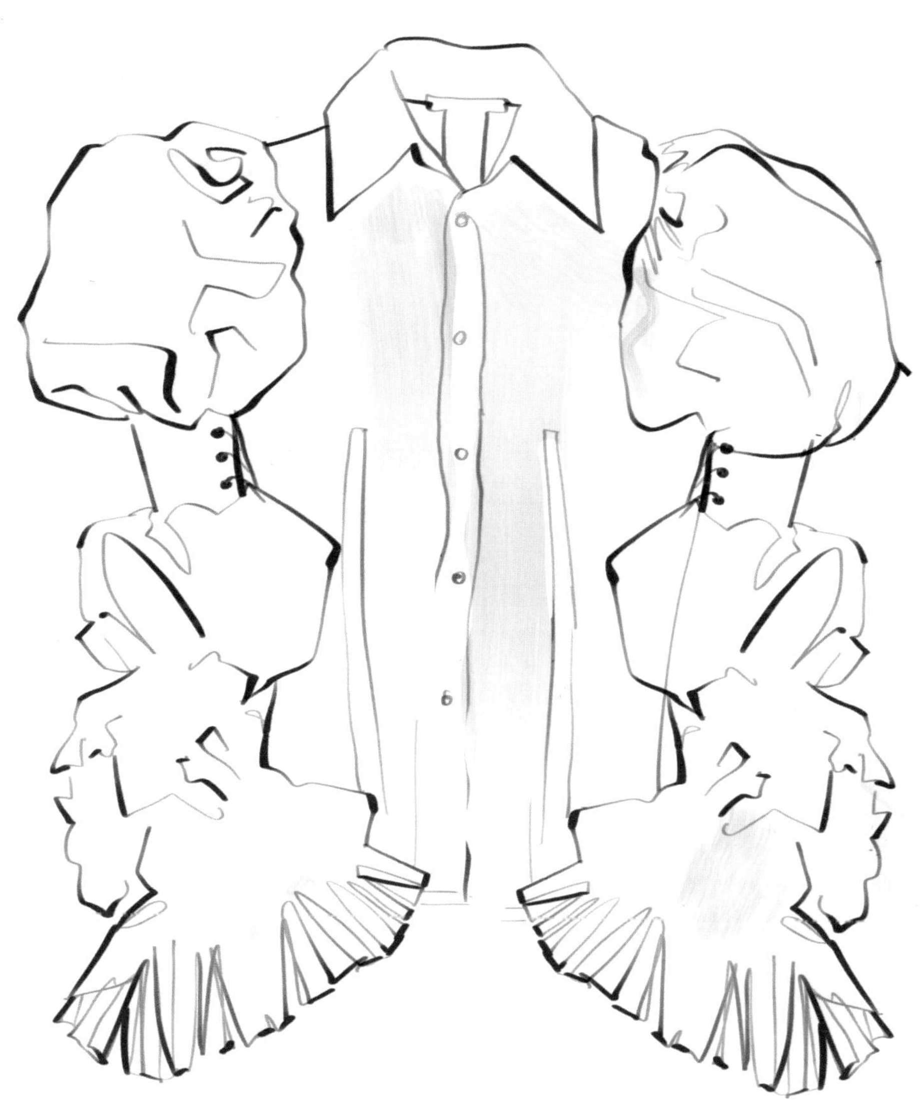

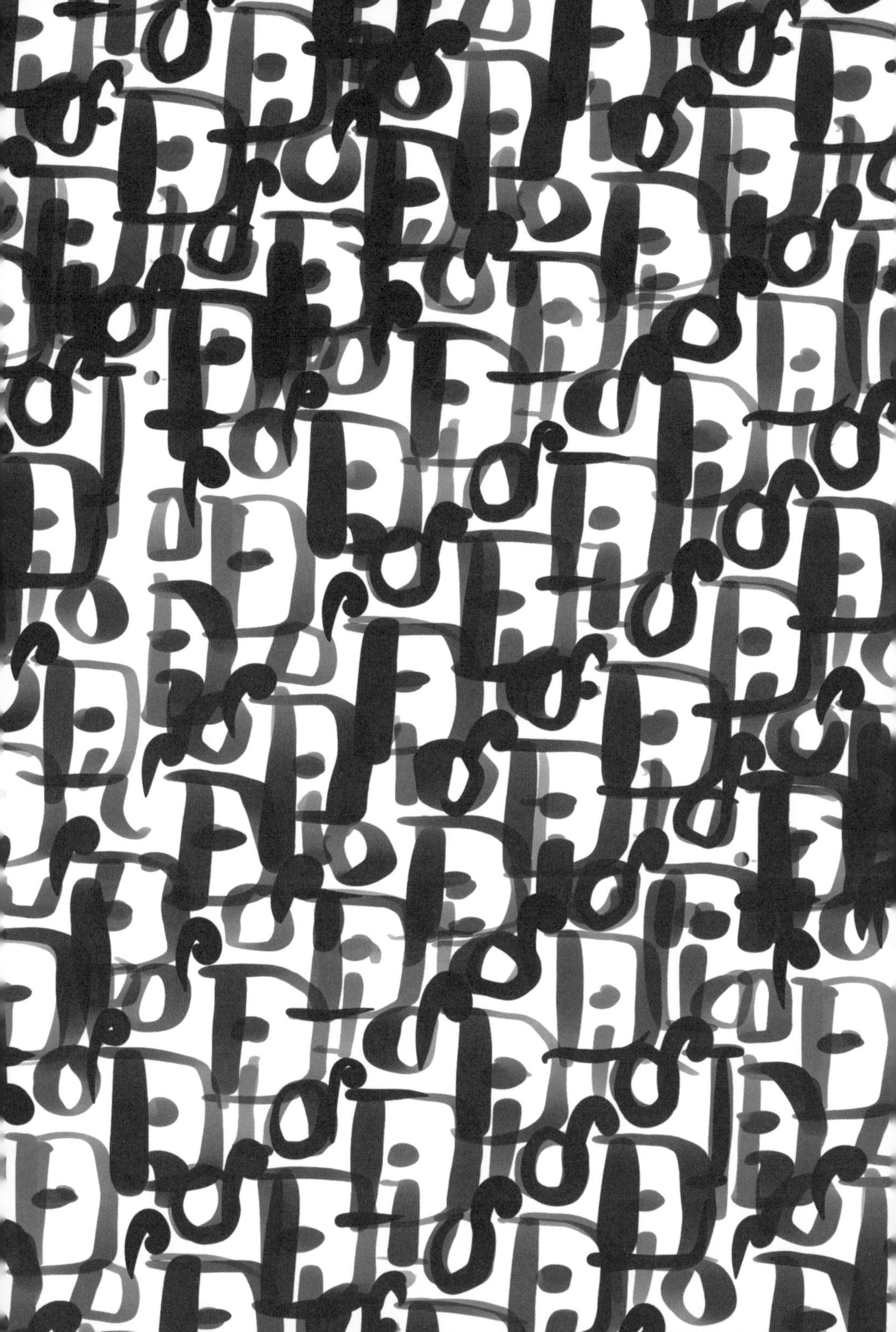

35

THE DIOR OBLIQUE PATTERN

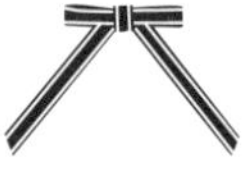

DATE: 1969

CREATED BY: MARC BOHAN

WORN BY: PARIS HILTON, MARIAH CAREY, MISSY ELLIOTT

In 1969, Dior unveiled a new pattern that would help define the fashion house's global identity for years to come. The "Dior Oblique" pattern was created by Marc Bohan two years earlier, taking its name from one of Christian Dior's collections from the 1950s. The design features the Dior insignia repeated to form an instantly recognizable pattern. It was initially featured on the label's handbags before moving on to luggage styles and, in 1974, the timeless 30 Montaigne boutique.

Fast forward to the 90s and John Galliano used the pattern to embellish everything from bikinis to bucket hats and handbags. Some of the biggest celebrities of the 00s were also known to sport the Dior monogram, including Paris Hilton, Mariah Carey and Missy Elliott. And as the fashion world gets nostalgic, the Dior Oblique has returned in full force, partly thanks to Kim Jones and Maria Grazia Chiuri, who showed much love for the look in their collections.

Jones won over plenty with both his homage to the classic and his maxi take on the motif, which he spread across much of the Dior menswear accessories range during this tenure – notably in footwear, where he pleased streetwear fans with his Nike Air Force One collab. Chiuri spoke to *Vogue* in 2018 on the famous print, saying, "It's the perfect graphic. It contains both logo and texture, both irony and seriousness, together in one. It is traditional, but at the same time has a pop sensibility."

36

THE PALLADIO DRESS

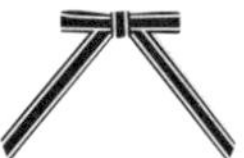

INSPIRATION: ANDREA PALLADIO,
ITALIAN RENAISSANCE ARCHITECT
AESTHETIC: ARCHITECTURAL AND GEOMETRIC SHAPES
TO MIMIC A GREEK PILLAR
STYLE: PUFF SLEEVES, TRIMMED NECKLINE
AND LONG, PLEATED SKIRT

Gianfranco Ferré's ability to bring elements of architecture into the world of fashion earned him immense respect as one of the world's most talented designers of the twentieth century. One of his most iconic pieces that would do just that is the "Palladio Dress" from his Dior spring/summer 1992 collection, entitled *From Balmy Summer Breezes*.

The pleated white silk design was inspired by a Greek pillar and took its name from an Italian Renaissance architect Andrea Palladio (1508–80) and his distinct architectural style. The gown's puff sleeves mimic the column's volutes, while the skirt aligns with the column's sheath. Admiration for the dress spread far and wide following its runway debut, with one of its most notable fans being Naoko Takeuchi, the creator of hit manga series *Sailor Moon*. The Palladio dress inspired Takeuchi to dress one of her key characters, Princess Serenity, in a lookalike style, introducing the garment to a whole new audience. The dress continues to be regarded as one of Dior's most widely recognized styles, by fans of the Japanese series and fashion lovers alike.

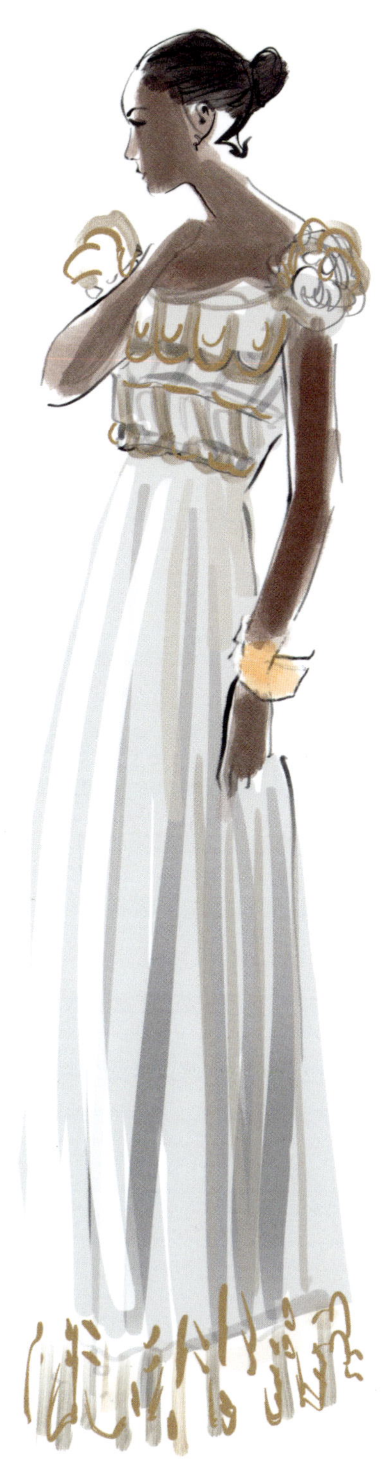

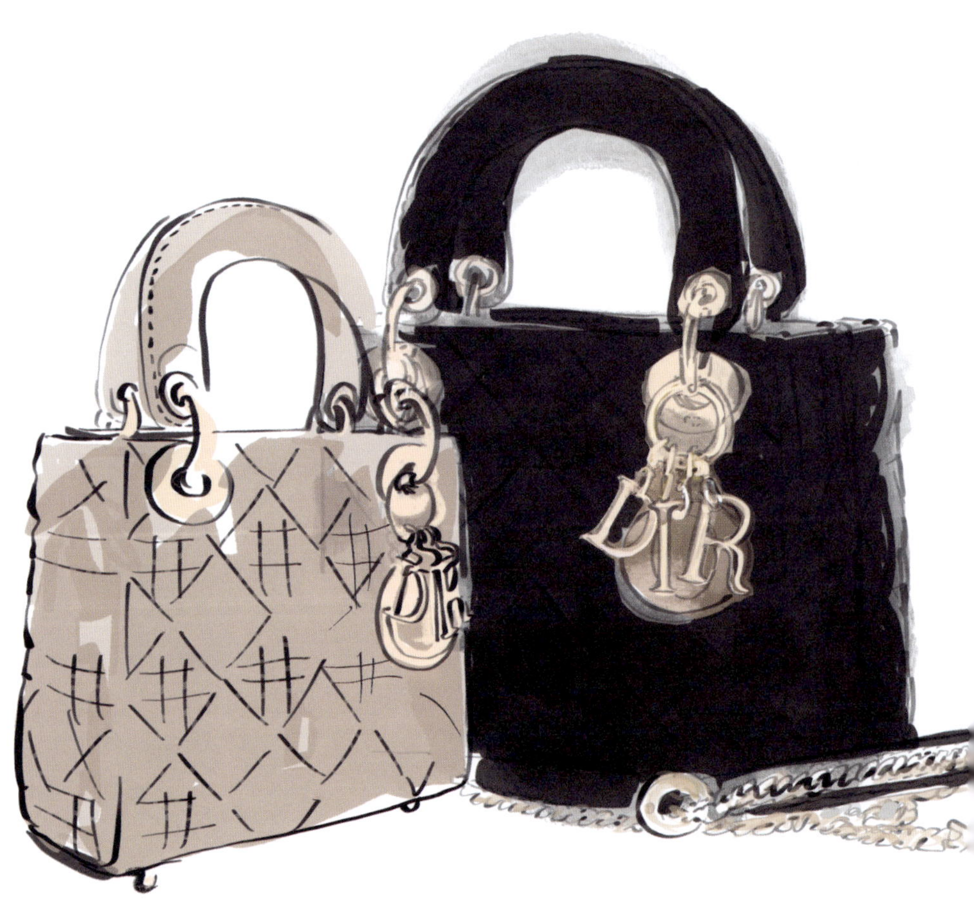

37

THE LADY DIOR

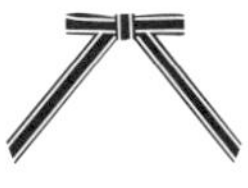

DATE: 1995

INCLUDES: CHARMS AS A REFERENCE TO DIOR'S SUPERSTITIONS

POPULARIZED BY (AND THEN RENAMED TO HONOUR): DIANA, PRINCESS OF WALES

The "Lady Dior" bag may not date back as far as some of the label's other iconic styles, but the story of how it came to be would likely make Christian Dior himself proud. The bag was originally designed by Gianfranco Ferré in the September of 1995 and was referred to simply as "Chouchou" ("favourite" in French). Ferré took inspiration from the Napoleon III-style cane chairs found in Dior's Paris couture salon for the bag's "cannage" stitching pattern, which mimicked the chairs' back panels. He is also said to have included hanging charms to reference Christian's tradition of infusing his designs with good-luck charms.

In 1995, Bernadette Chirac, then First Lady of France, saw the bag as the perfect gift for a special guest who would be attending the Paul Cézanne art exhibition in Paris – Diana, Princess of Wales. It's said that Diana loved the small quilted leather bag so much that she immediately requested the design in every colour. She would go on to wear the bag to a number of high-profile events, including the Met Gala in 1996.

Since finding its way into Diana's hands, all those years ago, the bag has been officially branded as the "Lady Dior bag" and continues to be seen as one of Dior's most iconic accessories. The design has been reinterpreted a number of times in countless colourways and modern updates but the original boxy, quilted leather style remains a staple in many Dior lovers' collections the world over.

38

DIOR HOMME SLIM SUITS

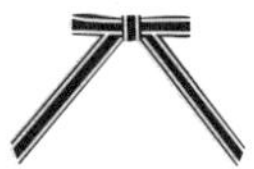

CREATED BY: HEDI SLIMANE
STYLE: SHARP CUTS AND SLIM SILHOUETTES
LEGACY: INFLUENCED MODERN MENSWEAR AND TAILORING

Though Dior had been creating menswear styles under the name Dior Monsieur since the 1980s, the impact of Dior's menswear output was amplified tenfold in 2001 when it was relaunched as Dior Homme, with Hedi Slimane appointed as creative director. Slimane had made a name for himself as artistic director at YSL, gaining attention for moving away from the oversized, structured menswear silhouettes of the 80s and 90s. But it would be at Dior Homme where Slimane's vision would truly come to life.

Slimane's first Dior Homme collection premiered on the runway in 2000 and quickly caused a stir in the world of menswear with its slim suiting looks, prompting fashion lovers to keep a close eye on the label's output. Over the next few years, Slimane would transform not only the label but menswear as a whole with his sharp cuts and skinny silhouettes, prompting *GQ*'s Lucy Kaylin to announce that "the sleek, chic style of Hedi Slimane has revolutionized manhood itself." In his 2004 book, Karl Lagerfield credits his 40 kilogram weight loss to Slimane's designs, sharing, "I suddenly wanted to wear the clothes designed by Hedi Slimane [...] but these fashions, modelled by very, very slim boys (and not men of my age) required me to lose at least 40 kilos." Slimane's contributions to Dior Homme continue to be regarded as some of menswear's most iconic looks and made way for a new era of androgynous dressing.

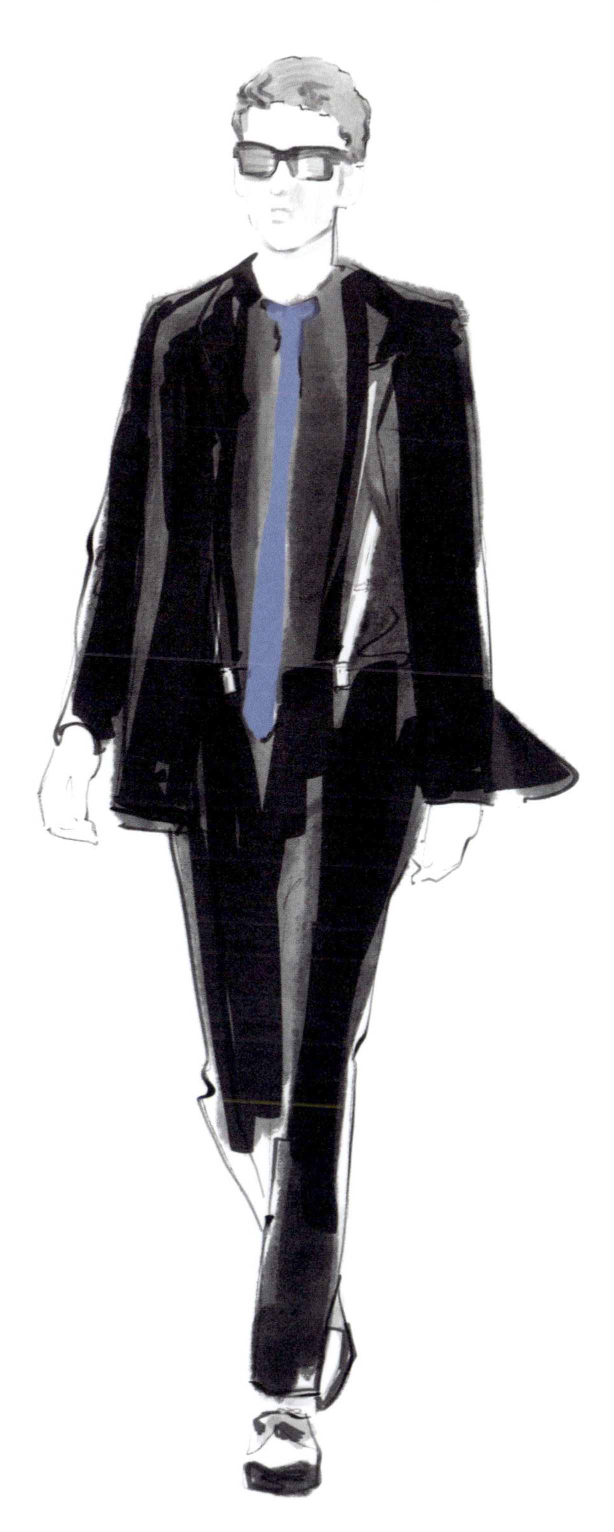

39

NEWSPAPER DRESS

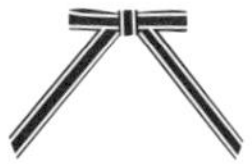

CREATED BY: JOHN GALLIANO
WORN BY: CARRIE BRADSHAW IN *SEX AND THE CITY*
LEGACY: THE DRESS NOW RESELLS FOR HUNDREDS OF THOUSANDS OF DOLLARS

Dior's connection to women on-screen continued into the new millennium with Sarah Jessica Parker wearing a newspaper-print dress in the 17th episode of Season 3 of *Sex and the City*, originally airing on 8 October 2000. The episode saw protagonist Carrie Bradshaw wearing the bias-cut slip-style design in the final scene with her famous narration reflecting on her recent decision to break up with the elusive Mr. Big. The dress became an instant hit with audiences, inspiring plenty of fast fashion copies soon after and a return to screens in the 2010 film, *Sex and the City 2*.

Another aspect that adds to the infamy of the dress was former creative director John Galliano's alleged inspiration behind the design being the homeless of Paris sleeping among newspapers, something that, according to *Harper's Bazaar*, was "criticised by many for appropriating poverty". The dress would cement itself as one of the *Sex and the City* series' most famous looks and a key look in Dior's catalogue of the era. In 2022, it was sold by Bonhams for 15,300 euros. By 2024, the estimated worth was rumoured to be over double that figure. And if you were unable to get your hands on the original version, there was one on vintage resale site 1stdibs for £203,278.16.

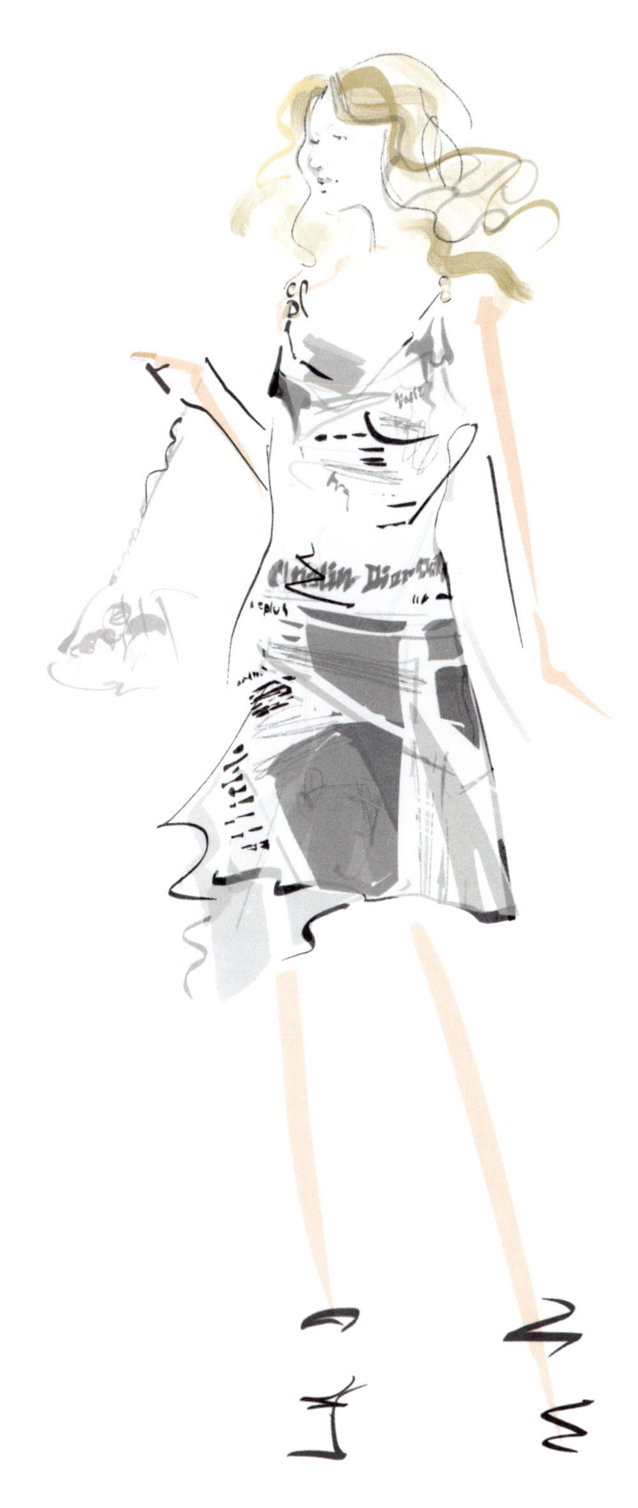

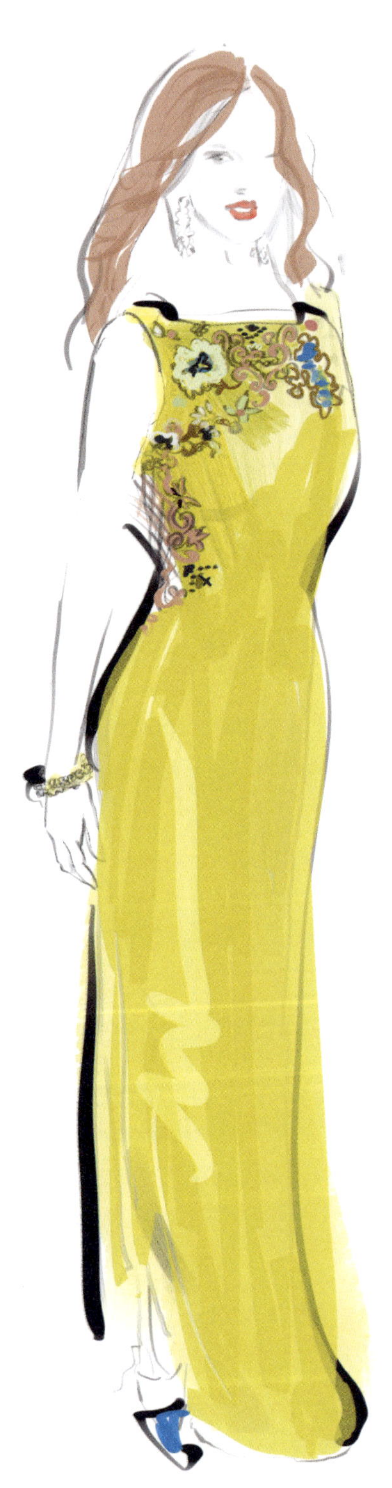

40

NICOLE KIDMAN'S OSCARS DRESS

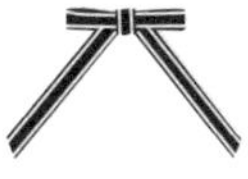

DATE: 1997
LOCATION: HOLLYWOOD, LOS ANGELES
MATERIAL: CHINOISERIE SILK WITH MINK LINING

Not long after John Galliano took the reins as Dior's creative director in October 1996, he would have the world talking about one particular chartreuse number worn by one of Hollywood's favourite leading ladies of the time. Nicole Kidman faced the red carpet with then-husband Tom Cruise wearing the chinoiserie look that was custom made for her, based on a design from the Dior spring/summer 1997 couture collection. This inspired strong reactions across the board, with talk-show host Joan Rivers notably showing disgust at the shade of the dress.

The infamous silk gown featured a statement mesh back panel, mink lining and side slits. At the time the dress would be the most expensive to be worn to the Oscars in its 67-year history. Not only would it be remembered for its price tag, but for its role in establishing Galliano's place in the fashion world and introducing the public to his controversial style.

When interviewed on the red carpet by fashion editor Merle Ginsberg, Kidman remarked that she was feeling nervous about whether or not people would "get" the look, before going on to state confidently, "But if they don't, well, maybe they should."

The dress continues to be regarded as one of the most iconic looks in the history of the Oscars, winning it a spot at *The House of Dior: Seventy Years of Haute Couture* exhibition at the National Gallery of Victoria in Melbourne, Australia, in 2017.

41

PRINCESS DIANA'S MET GALA DRESS

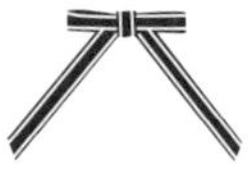

DATE: 1996

LOCATION: NEW YORK CITY

SYMBOLIZED: DIANA BREAKING FREE OF HER ROYAL IMAGE

Less than a year before her death in a car crash in Paris, Princess Diana attended an event that would confirm her status as a true style icon. The 1996 Met Gala showcased some of the biggest stars of the time dressed to pay homage to Christian Dior himself. The story goes that Diana approached John Galliano to adapt an existing dress from the designer's first Dior collection for her to wear to the event. Galliano claims that he was pushing for the late princess to agree to the dress in a pink hue that was representative of the Dior name but she had her sights set on a deep navy. It's also rumoured that Diana was concerned about the level of reveal that the dress boasted, as her son William was 14 at the time and he might feel embarrassed. Ultimately, though, she decided to go with it. The slip-style dress was worn with a matching robe, statement jewels and her "Lady Dior" handbag.

Galliano recalled the night of the event in an episode of the 2024 documentary series *In Vogue: The 90s*: "Fast-forward to the event and I just remember her getting out of the car. I couldn't believe it. She'd ripped the corset out. She didn't want to wear the corset." This revelation added even more acclaim to the already iconic look that helped pull Diana away from the timid woman we once knew and who, as *Vogue* wrote, "was enjoying a new phase of her life unshackled from Kensington Palace protocol", following her divorce that same year.

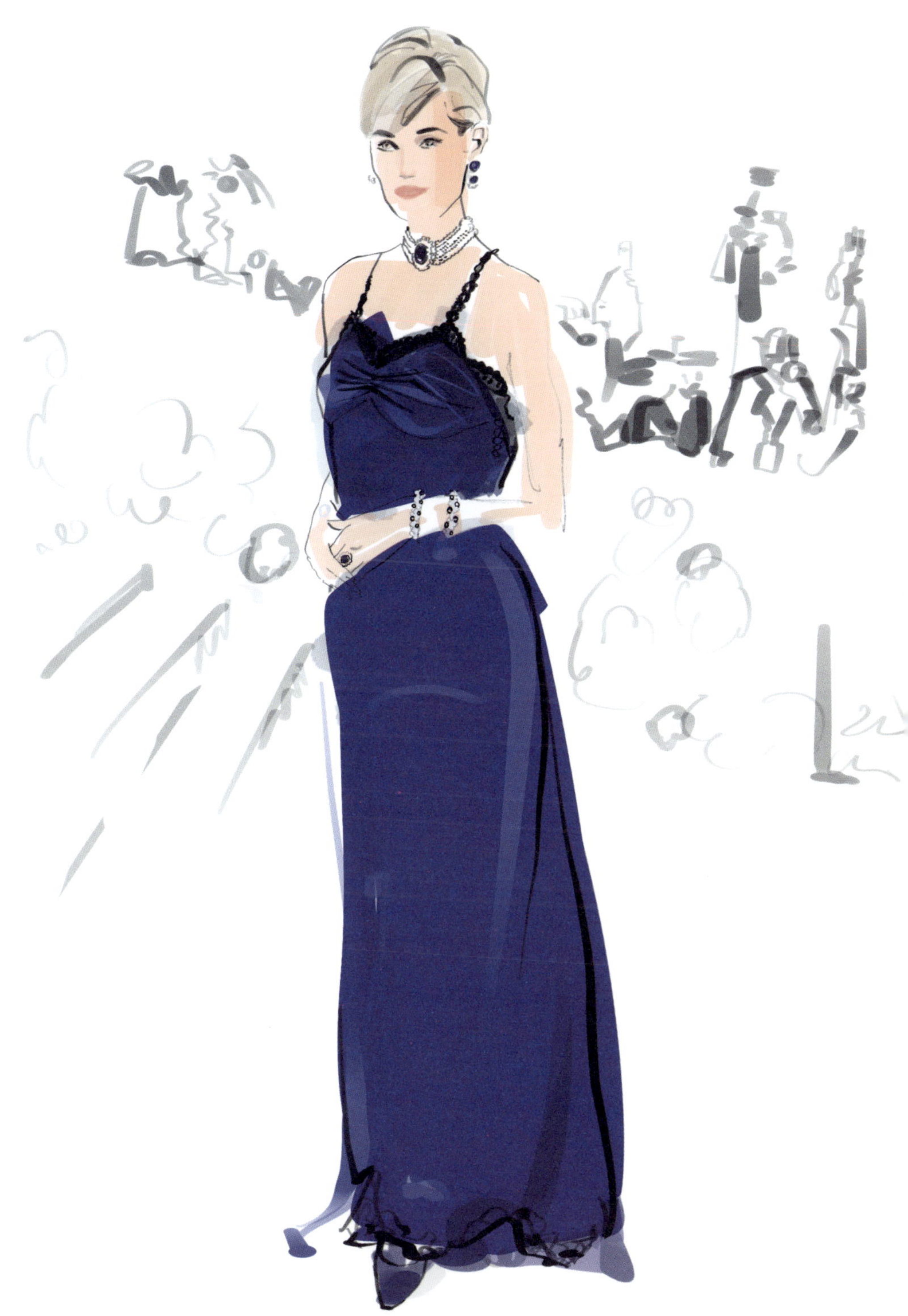

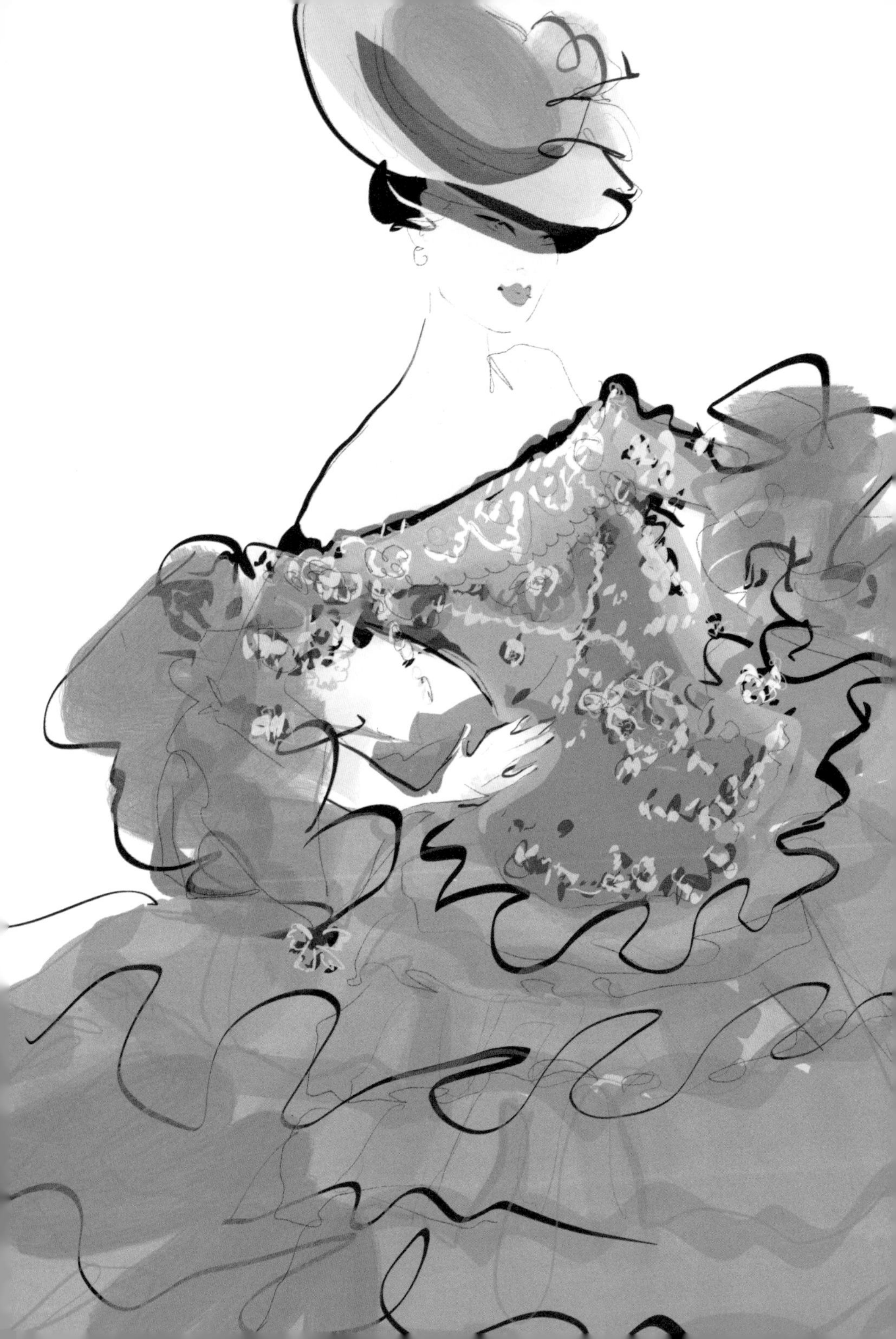

42

GALLIANO'S GOWNS

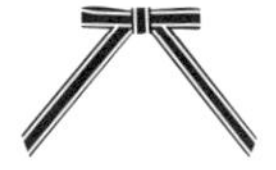

DATE: 1997–2011
INSPIRATION: ART, OPERA, BALLET
DESIGNS: BIG, EXTREME AND DRAMATIC

John Galliano's tenure at Dior can easily be defined by the British designer's affinity for extremes. "From Madame Butterfly, to Versailles, to Opera Garnier, Galliano staged heart-racing odysseys of escapee princesses and gypsy queens," *Dazed*'s senior fashion writer Daniel Rodgers once wrote on the designer's Dior runway shows. And the only thing to meet this top-tier drama would be Galliano's gowns themselves, which – from his first Dior collection for spring/summer 1997 – would become talking points across the fashion world. Some of the best examples can be found in the Dior autumn/winter 2005 collection, where the line-up featured dramatic cuts and ruffles crafted from organza, influenced by the rich heritage of the French fashion house and its founder.

The autumn/winter 2007 collection marked the 60th anniversary of the House of Dior, and Galliano used it as an opportunity to go big with his designs and presentation. The gowns that graced the Versailles catwalk were said to have been partly inspired by the work of impressionists such as Claude Monet and Pierre-Auguste Renoir, alongside those that Christian Dior counted among his friends (Jean Cocteau, Pablo Picasso and René Gruau). Throughout his career Galliano has noted influences ranging from ancient Egypt to the Ballets Russes, resulting in texturally rich collections that continue to fascinate young designers and fashion anthropologists across the globe. Galliano's time at Dior came to a dramatic end in 2011 when he was dismissed following allegations he had made antisemitic remarks, for which he was subsequently convicted.

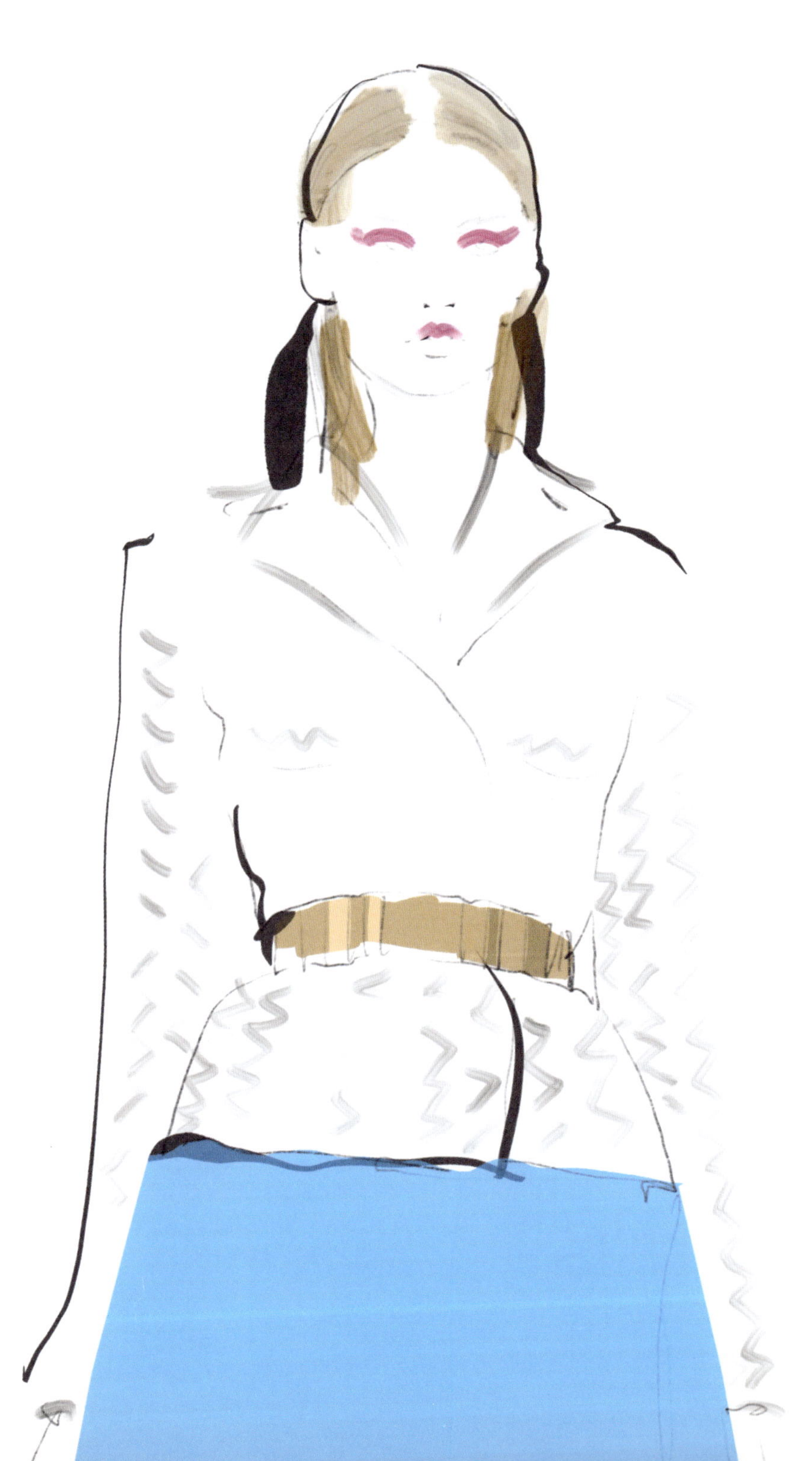

43

RAF SIMONS' NEW LOOK

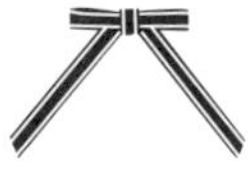

DATE: 2011

REINTRODUCED: PARED BACK ELEGANCE AND SLEEK DESIGN

DESIGNS: THE COAT-DRESS, FULL SKIRTS WITH MODEST BODICES

When the Belgian designer Raf Simons joined Dior as creative director in 2011, he is said to have remarked to *Vogue*, "I want to make it more dynamic and appeal to a person who has a different energy – a younger person, in mind, not necessarily in age."

According to the reports from critics who caught his first collection for the French fashion house, he succeeded in doing just that. The Dior autumn/winter 2012 collection moved away from the extravagant style that his predecessor John Galliano had infused into each of his Dior designs, and refocused on the dedication to stark lines and pared-back elegance on which Christian Dior had based the house's foundations. One of the key pieces of the season was a red coat-dress that instantly drew comparisons to the Bar Suit from Dior's 1947 collection, inspiring the "New Look" title due to its fresh take on the feminine silhouette. Alongside this striking style, the collection offered a selection of gowns in modest bodices and full skirts, contrasted by slim suiting looks. Together, the styles formed a line-up signalling a new age of Dior with a fresh approach that balanced modern innovations with traditional tones in a way that only Raf Simons could execute.

44

JENNIFER LAWRENCE, ACADEMY AWARDS DRESS, 2013

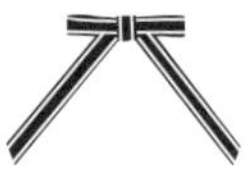

DATE: 2013

STYLE: STRAPLESS BODICE, DROP WAIST AND BILLOWING SKIRT

MATERIAL: PALE PINK SILK BROCADE

One of Raf Simons' most noteworthy looks from his time at Dior would be a pale pink gown from the spring 2013 couture collection, characterized by its strapless style, dropped waist and billowing skirt. The look would be plastered across news sites following the 85th Academy Awards, where rising star Jennifer Lawrence fell victim to the dress's train, tripping as she climbed the stairs to collect her award for Best Actress for her role in *Silver Linings Playbook* (2012).

"Nevertheless, the glowing-with-glamour Lawrence coped and the teeny mishap made her into even more of a Hollywood sweetheart," wrote fashion journalist Natasha Fraser-Cavassoni. This would prove to be a key moment in the American actress's rise to fame and would mark the first of Simons' red-carpet successes during his brief tenure at Dior.

Lawrence would continue to sport exclusively Dior for her red-carpet appearances for the next few years, as well as starring in plenty of Dior campaigns, including Miss Dior in 2013. The infamous brocade number took notes from Christian Dior's affinity for shapes that mimic florals, with Simons later saying in the show notes for spring/summer 2014 couture that he was aiming to create a "new tribe of flower women", paraphrasing Christian's own words from 1948.

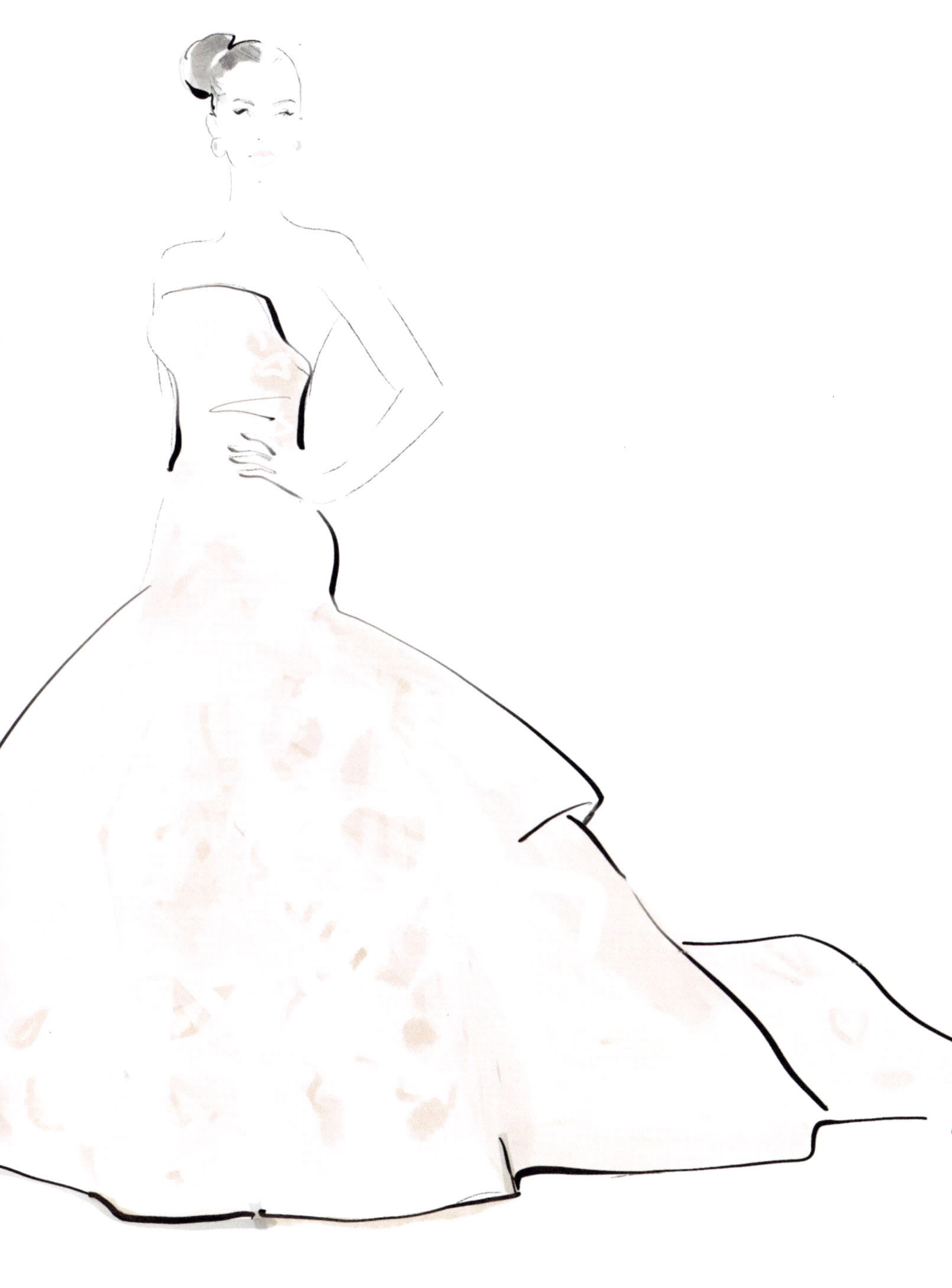

45

STEPHEN JONES

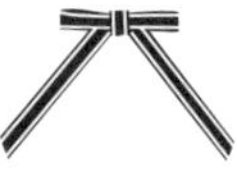

DATE: 1996–PRESENT
KEY DESIGNS: RED CORSETED TOP HAT, GLASS AND RESIN SEAHORSE CROWN, EMBROIDERED SUEDE PALETTE HAT
SIGNIFICANCE: FIRST BRITISH MILLINER TO DESIGN FOR DIOR

Though Christian Dior's love for hats dates back much further than his 1954 *Little Dictionary of Fashion*, one of the maison's millinery department's biggest moments didn't occur until 1996 when Stephen Jones joined forces with then-artistic director John Galliano. The hat-maker was the first Brit to hold the position at Dior and quickly gained respect with his incredible headwear pieces.

By the time he joined Dior, Jones had been studying and admiring Dior's designs for decades as he cut his teeth at fellow couture houses. As Galliano pushed limits with his extravagant looks, Jones created headpieces to match (notably a metre-tall, gilded column for Dior's spring/summer 2004 couture show, which he lists as one of his all-time favourite designs). When artistic director Kim Jones entered Dior Men (then Dior Homme) in 2018, Jones was there to offer plenty of bowler hats and berets to complement his collections.

"Stephen has been the milliner to Christian Dior for 25 years – for me, he is the brand's oracle. He has absorbed all its facets, and all those of a couturier too," Kim remarked about Stephen in the 260-page book, *Dior Hats: From Christian Dior to Stephen Jones* (2020).

In 2022, the Musée Christian Dior in Granville, Normandy, hosted a dazzling exhibition which followed the same theme with a selection of sketches and magazine clippings that displayed Jones' creations alongside around 200 hat designs.

"Without hats there is no civilization"

Christian Dior, *Little Dictionary of Fashion*

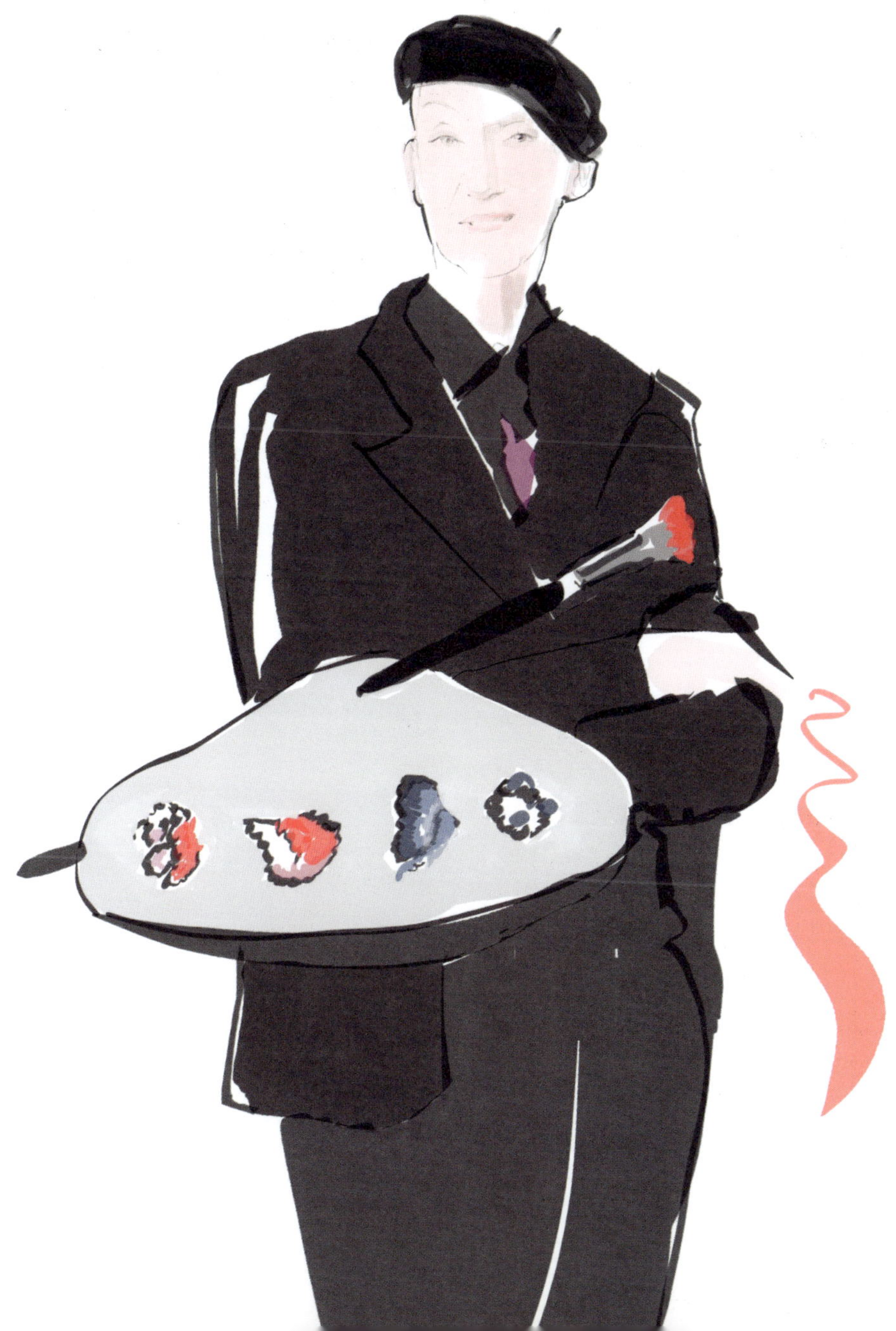

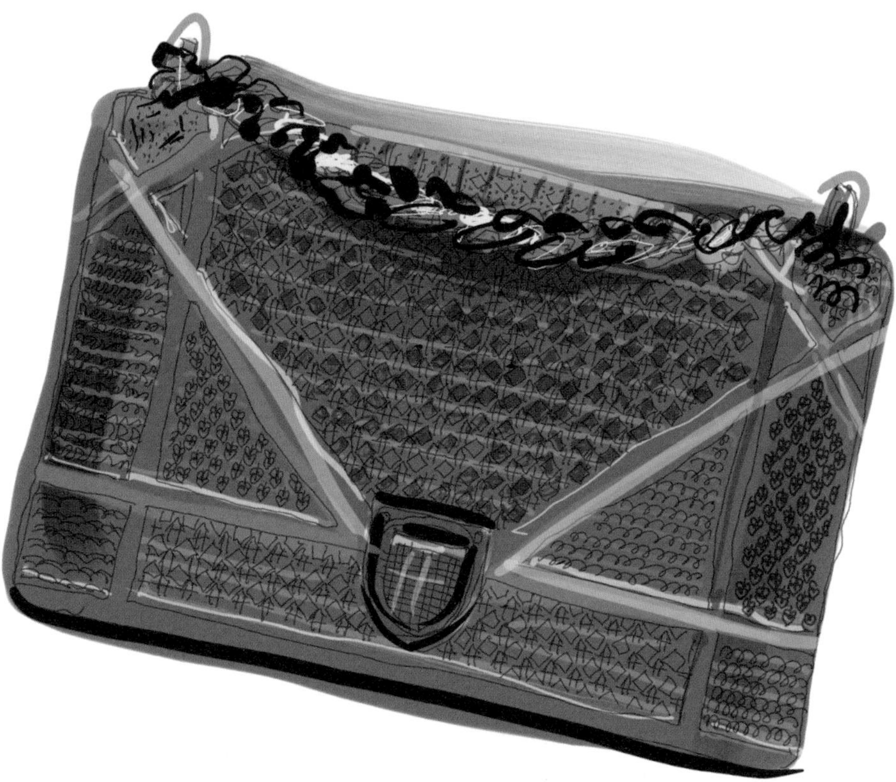

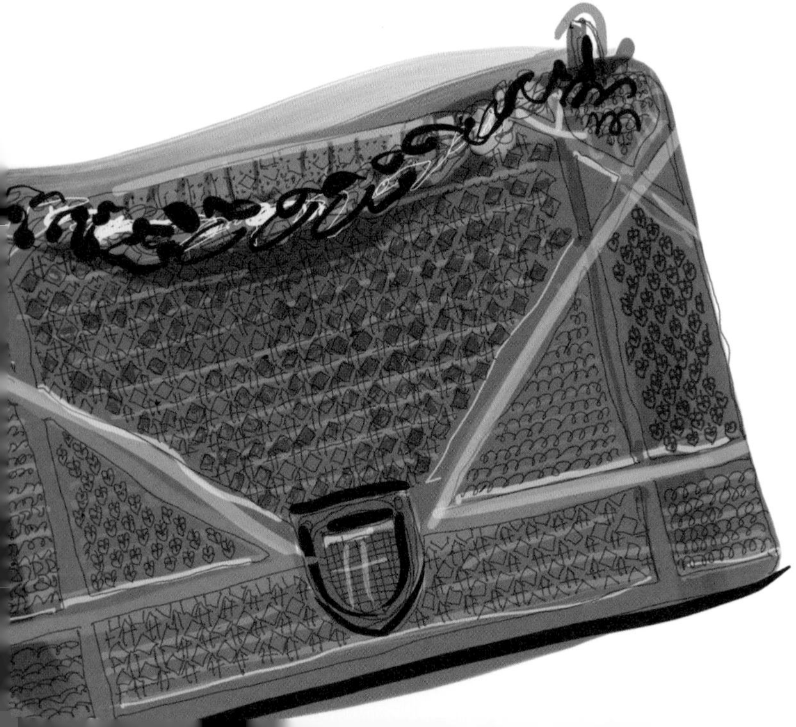

46

THE DIOR DIORAMA

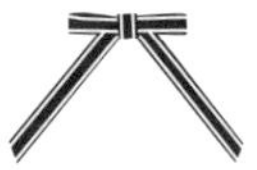

DATE: 2015–2020
MATERIALS: SMOOTH OR EMBOSSED LEATHER WITH A CHAIN STRAP
WORN BY: RIHANNA, BELLA HADID, MARION COTILLARD

In 2015, creative director Raf Simons introduced a handbag to the world that would embody a shift from the traditional into the modern for the French fashion house's handbag designs. The "Dior Diorama" is defined by its structured shape, flat closure and chain strap. The first iterations were presented on the runway in Paris as part of the Dior spring/summer 2015 ready-to-wear collection in both smooth leather and embossed styles and a range of colourways that fitted with the collection's futuristic mood. Alongside these models, we were also introduced to the house's iconic "cannage" embossing that continues to be a key reference across a range of its outputs.

Since its debut, the Dior Diorama continues to be a favourite among high-profile fans, including French actress Marion Cotillard and British singer-songwriter and actress Pixie Lott. Rihanna has also been spotted on multiple occasions with the handbag since making history as Dior's first Black ambassador for the brand in 2015.

Though the House of Dior ceased to produce the bag in 2020, the Diorama continues to be a coveted design and is popular among premium resale sites online, encouraging collectors everywhere to obtain their own piece of Dior history.

47

THE TOTE BAG

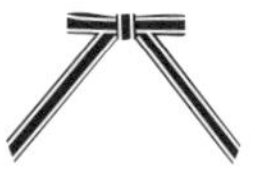

DATE: 2018
DESIGN: RECTANGULAR SHAPE IN JACQUARD CANVAS, DISPLAYING THE FULL NAME OF THE BRAND
IMPACT: IT HAS BECOME AN ICONIC AND HIGHLY SOUGHT-AFTER PIECE FOR FASHION LOVERS

Throughout her tenure at Dior, creative director Maria Grazia Chiuri demonstrated an incredible ability to identify pieces that make quite an impact. The introduction of the "Dior Book Tote" in 2018 is a true testament to that power. Though she credits Marc Bohan with originally creating the bag in the 1960s, Chiuri is said to have rescued the once-forgotten style and introduced it to the Dior catalogue as a part of her spring/summer 2018 collection.

The style is defined by its rectangular shape that lends itself perfectly to the middle stripe that displays the full name of the French fashion house's founder across the jacquard canvas construction. Since then, the humble design has become synonymous with some of the world's hottest stars and has been reimagined in plenty of materials, colourways and sizes, including a leather number that mimics a cannage design, a mini cross-body style and the classic carry-all model with the "Dior Oblique" pattern. The structured style and size of the original rendition situates it among the more practical of Dior's handbag designs, cementing its spot among the top coveted pieces for fashion lovers around the world.

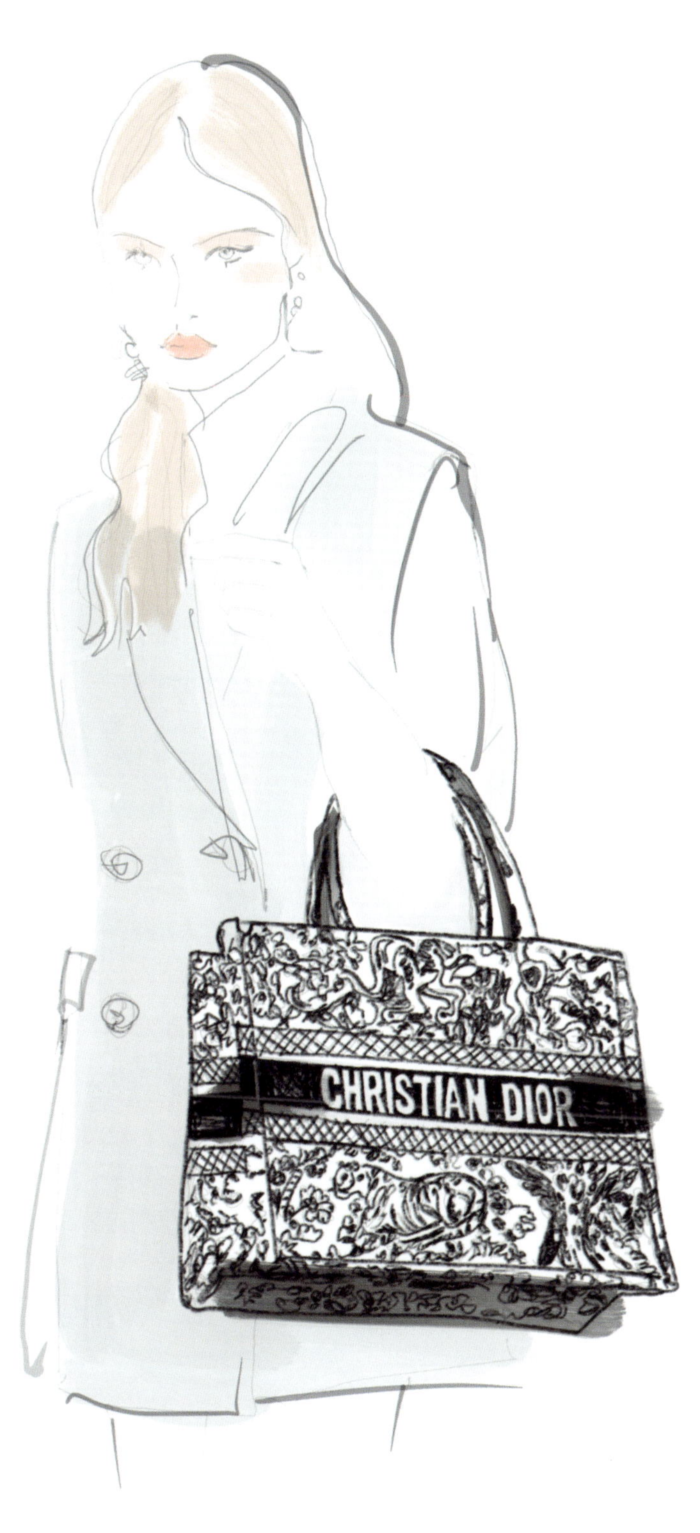
CHRISTIAN DIOR

48

MARIA GRAZIA'S STATEMENT TEES

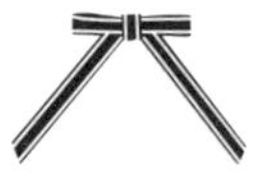

DATE: 2016

INSPIRATION: QUOTES REFERENCED FROM CHIMAMANDA NGOZI ADICHIE, LINDA NOCHLIN

IMPACT: BECAME A FAVOURITE OF DIOR FANS AND SENT A STATEMENT AS PART OF CHIURI'S FIRST COLLECTION

Marking her arrival in the coveted artistic director role at Dior, the Italian designer Maria Grazia Chiuri made headlines with her spring/summer 2016 show showcasing a white tee that read "We Should All Be Feminists" paired with a floor-length tulle skirt with signature Dior embroidery. This statement was borrowed from a similarly titled TEDx Talk by Nigerian author and activist Chimamanda Ngozi Adichie, who was approached by Chiuri ahead of the collection. When asked why she was keen to work with Dior, Adichie shared, "A T-shirt is not going to change the world, right? But, I think change happens when we spread ideas."

The "We Should All Be Feminists" tee went on to become a favourite for Dior fans, including the likes of Jennifer Lawrence, Rihanna and Natalie Portman, who have all been photographed sporting the statement style. A portion of the sales of the tee was donated to Rihanna's charity, the Clara Lionel Foundation, which aims to support access to education and fight impacts of climate change across the globe.

Chiuri's next collection followed the same statement tee theme, with the opening look featuring: "Why Have There Been No Great Women Artists?" (in reference to Linda Nochlin's 1971 feminist essay) across a striped long-sleeved tee.

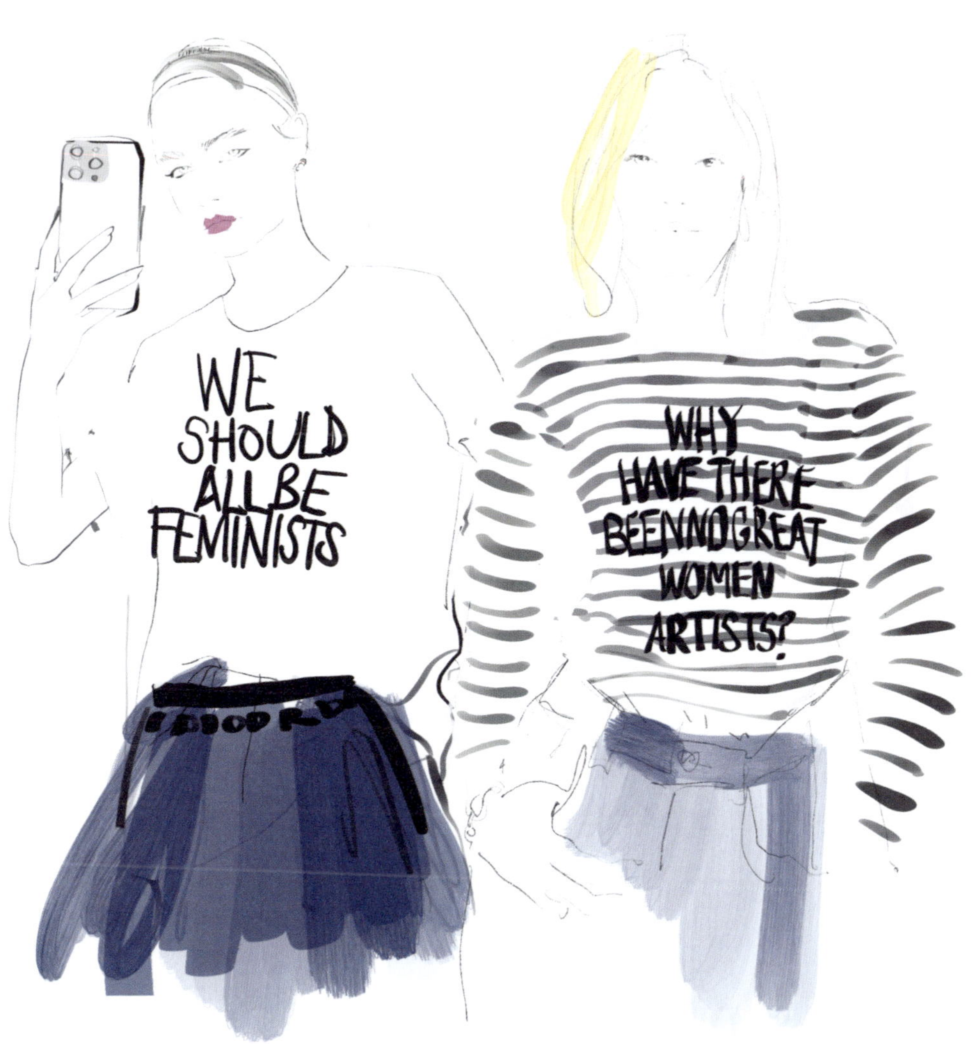
WE
SHOULD
ALL BE
FEMINISTS
WHY
HAVE THERE
BEEN NO GREAT
WOMEN
ARTISTS?

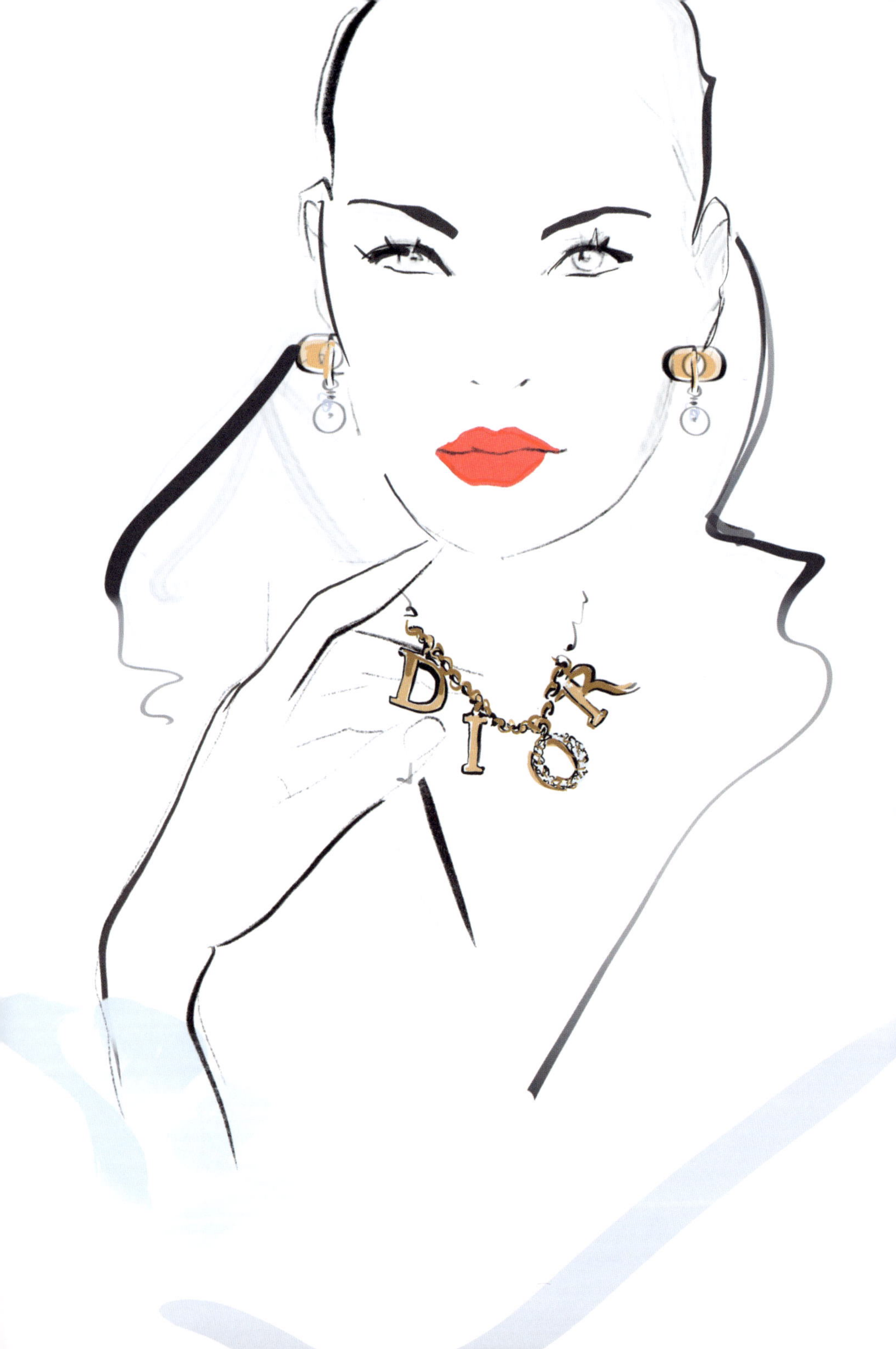
DIOR

49

LOGO JEWELLERY

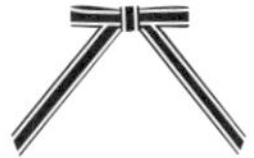

DESIGNS: OFFERS BOLDER MEDALLION STYLES AS WELL AS THE SIMPLE CD LOGO FOR MORE ELEGANT LOOKS
COLLABORATIONS: SWAROVSKI, ROBERT GOOSSENS AND ROGER JEAN-PIERRE
IMPACT: SETTING DIOR APART FROM OTHER FASHION HOUSES, THE BRAND HAS ALWAYS OFFERED MORE THAN JUST CLOTHES

In his 1954 book, *The Little Dictionary of Fashion*, Christian Dior stated, "As a rule I would use jewellery generously to get the most out of it. A many stoned necklace of rhinestones for instance will look lovely with a décolleté frock for evening. It will go equally with a fine black knitted sweater for afternoons." Christian was known for always seeking to provide more than just clothing for his clients, but offering a full "top-to-toe" look – and jewellery was integral to this vision. Despite the various directions in which the Dior brand has gone, honouring Christian Dior's love for jewellery has always remained a key part of the label's output.

Over the years the House of Dior has worked with a number of jewellery manufacturers to help bring its creations to life, from household names like Swarovski to boutique artisans such as Robert Goossens. The Dior jewellery range has always been a prime template for the Dior name to shine, with bolder medallion styles becoming a fan favourite through the 80s before being stripped back in the 90s. For many, the CD signature acts as one of the preferred logo looks due to its elegance and simplicity, illustrated here.

50

KIM JONES' PROPORTIONS

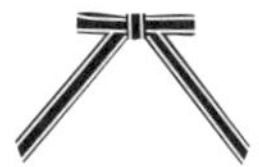

DATES: 2018–2025

SIGNIFICANCE: STEERED DIOR MEN IN A NEW DIRECTION AWAY FROM SLEEK AND SLIM SILHOUETTES

DESIGNS: CROPPED AND BOXY CUTS WITH LOOSER SILHOUETTES

When Kim Jones joined Dior Men (then Dior Homme) as artistic director in 2018, he told *The New York Times*, "I think it's time to do something new. [...] I want to surprise people with what I do." And, looking back on his time at the maison, it's fair to say he did just that.

Jones' impact on the world of menswear can be particularly felt in his playful take on proportions. Positioned between his hit streetwear-inspired designs (including the Dior x Air Jordan 1, which sent folk into a frenzy upon its release in 2020), Jones' tailored styles would go on to inspire a fresh approach to menswear that opened the door to new shapes for modern men everywhere. As early as his runway show for Dior Men pre-fall 2019 show in Tokyo, the change in tide could be felt with looser silhouettes emerging, moving away from the house's famous slim look. By 2024, Jones had truly carved out his legacy with the French fashion house through his reimagined silhouettes.

"I was looking at the idea of couture length in the twenties, at the dresses, but then making it as a trouser [...] So it's a new proportion for men," he told Samuel Hine, global fashion correspondent for *GQ*, regarding the Dior Men spring/summer 2024 collection looks. The boxy, cropped cuts helped pave the way for a new era of dressing for sartorially inclined men, for which we have Jones to thank.

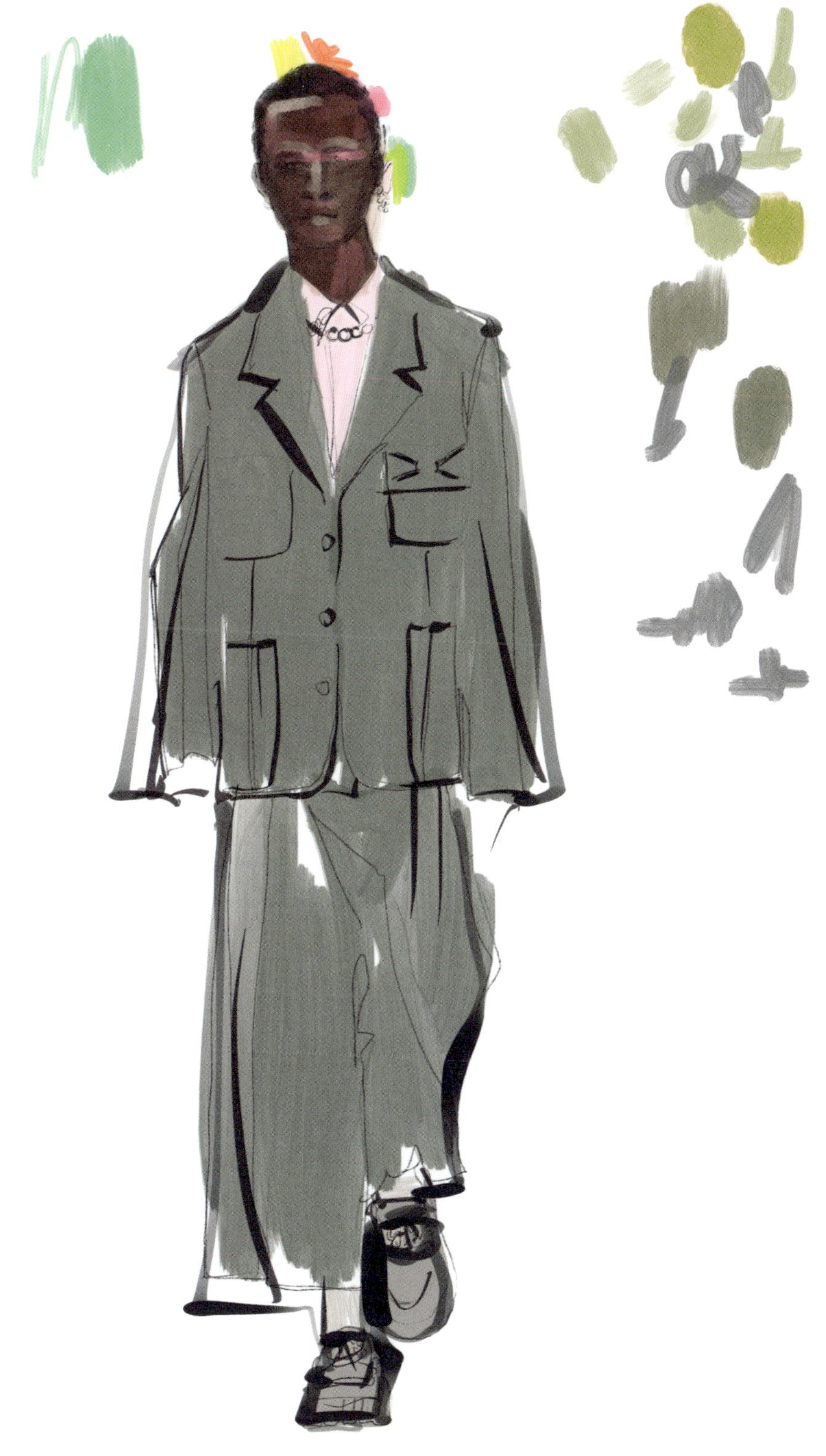

"MY DREAM?
TO MAKE
WOMEN
HAPPIER
AND MORE
BEAUTIFUL"

– Christian Dior

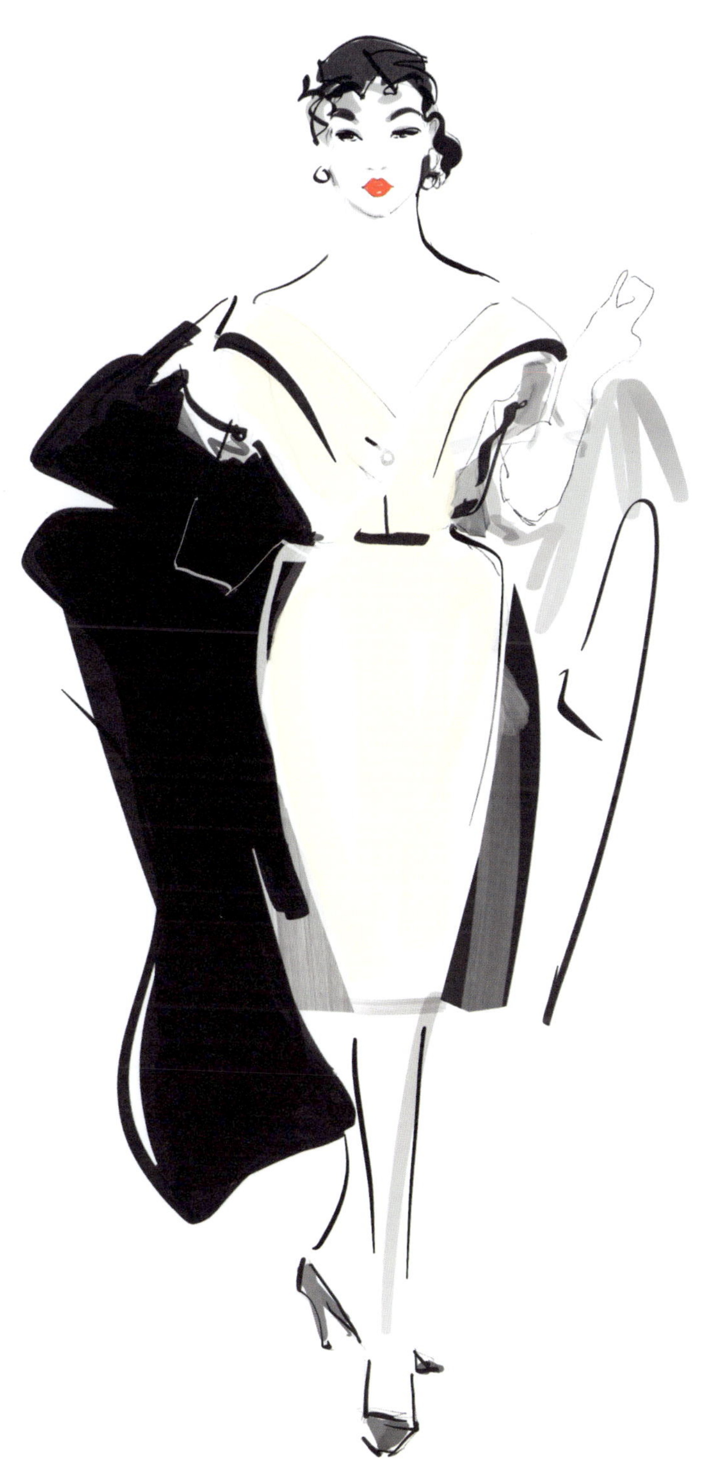

INDEX

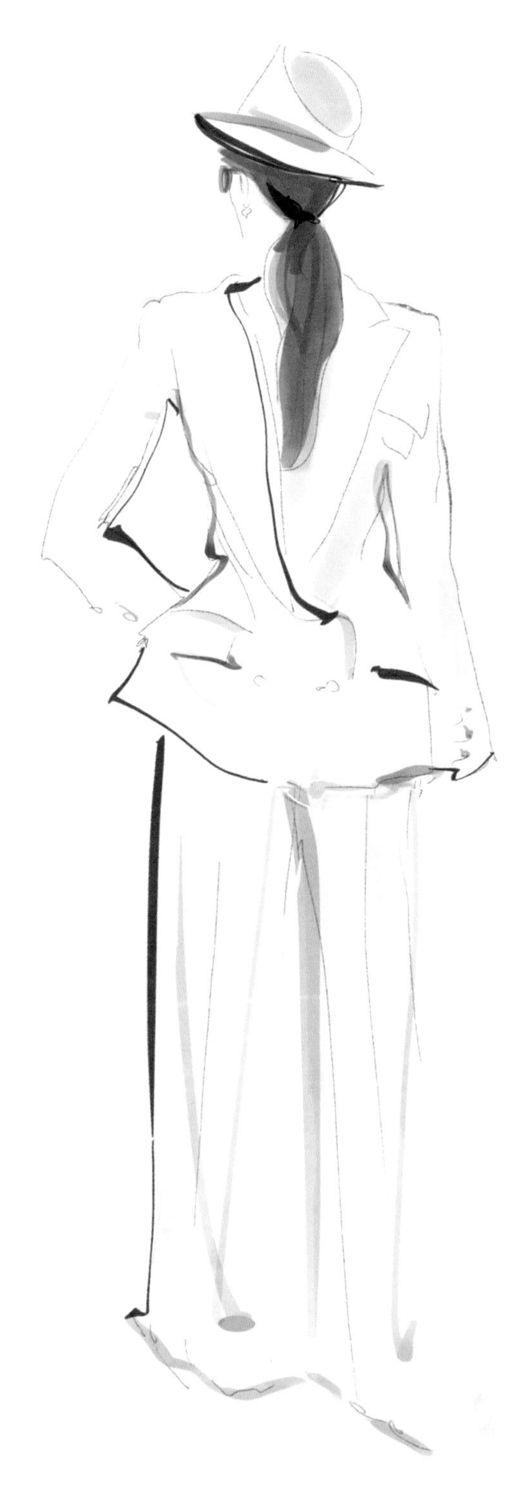